the
information 📞01603 773114
store email: tis@ccn.ac.uk

21 DAY LOAN ITEM

Adolescer

Please return <u>on or before</u> the last date stamped above

A fine will be charged for overdue items

CITY
COLLEGE
NORWICH

companion volumes

The Early Years
Assessing and Promoting Resilience in Vulnerable Children 1
Brigid Daniel and Sally Wassell
ISBN 1 84310 013 4

The School Years
Assessing and Promoting Resilience in Vulnerable Children 2
Brigid Daniel and Sally Wassell
ISBN 1 84310 018 5

Set of three workbooks
ISBN 1 84310 045 2

of related interest

Child Development for Child Care and Protection Workers
Brigid Daniel, Sally Wassell and Robbie Gilligan
ISBN 1 85302 633 6

The Child's World
Assessing Children in Need
Edited by Jan Horwath
ISBN 1 85302 957 2

Approaches to Needs Assessment in Children's Services
Edited by Harriet Ward and Wendy Rose
ISBN 1 85302 780 4

Social Work with Children and Families
Getting into Practice
Ian Butler and Gwenda Roberts
ISBN 1 85302 365 5

Creating a Safe Place
Helping Children and Families Recover from Child Sexual Abuse
NCH Children and Families Project
ISBN 1 84310 009 6

Adolescence

Assessing and Promoting Resilience in Vulnerable Children 3

Brigid Daniel and Sally Wassell
Illustrated by Iain Campbell

Jessica Kingsley Publishers
London and Philadelphia

First published in the United Kingdom in 2002
by Jessica Kingsley Publishers Ltd
116 Pentonville Road
London N1 9JB, England
and
325 Chestnut Street
Philadelphia, PA 19106, USA

www.jkp.com

Copyright © 2002 Brigid Daniel and Sally Wassell

Illustrations © 2002 Iain Campbell

Library of Congress Cataloging in Publication Data

A CIP catalog record for this book is available from the Library of Congress

British Library Cataloguing in Publication Data

A CIP catalogue record for this book is available from the British Library

ISBN 1 84310 019 3

Printed and Bound in Great Britain by
Athenaeum Press, Gateshead, Tyne and Wear

Contents

Acknowledgements   7

1   Introduction to Resilience   9

    Domains of Resilience   14

    Summary of Factors Associated with Resilience
      during Adolescent Years   15

2   When and How to Use the Workbook   17

Part I Assessment

3   Secure Base   27

    Secure Base Checklist: Young Person   30

    Secure Base Checklist: Parent/Carer   34

    Quality of Attachment   36

4   Education   37

    Education Checklist: Young Person   40

    Education Checklist: Parent/Carer   42

5   Friendships   45

    Friendships Checklist: Young Person   49

    My Friends and Me as a Friend   51

    Friendships Checklist: Parent/Carer   53

6   Talents and Interests   55

    Talents and Interests Checklist: Young Person   58

    What Can I Do and What Would I Like To Do?   60

    Self-Esteem   61

    Talents And Interests Checklist: Parent/Carer   63

7   Positive Values   65

        Positive Values Checklist: Young Person   69

        Moral Dilemma   73

        Emotional Faces   74

        Emotional Scenes   78

        An Index of Empathy for Children and Adolescents   83

        Positive Values Checklist: Parent/Carer   87

8   Social Competencies   89

        Social Competencies Checklist: Young Person   93

        Social Attributes Checklist   96

        Internal/External Locus of Control Scale   98

        Social Competencies Checklist: Parent/Carer   100

Part II Intervention

9   Intervention Strategies   105

        Practice Suggestions: Secure Base   107

        Practice Suggestions: Education   120

        Practice Suggestions: Friendships   127

        Practice Suggestions: Talents and Interests   132

        Practice Suggestions: Positive Values   141

        Practice Suggestions: Social Competencies   146

10   Case Studies   156

        Alison, aged 13   156

        Tom, aged 15   158

     Appendix: Moral Reasoning Stages   160

     Bibliography   163

     Subject Index   167

     Author Index   172

Acknowledgements

The writing and production of these workbooks was financially supported by the Social Work Services Inspectorate of the Scottish Executive. We would like to thank practitioners who helped to develop the material in these workbooks from Perth Social Work Department, Maryhill Social Work Centre, Glasgow and Children's Centres in North Edinburgh. We would also like to thank Robbie Gilligan, Professor of Social Work and Social Policy, and Director, Children's Research Centre, Trinity College, Dublin, and Jim Ennis, Elaine Ennis and Amelia Wilson of the Centre for Child Care and Protection Studies, Department of Social Work, University of Dundee for conceptual development and Helen Wosu for detailed comments. We are also extremely grateful to Stacey Farmer for administrative support. Thanks also to Christine Henderson and David Willshaw for support and encouragement.

Some of the issues in the workbooks have previously been published in Daniel, B., Wassell, S. and Gilligan, R. (1999) '"It's just common sense isn't it?": Exploring ways of putting the theory of resilience into action.' *Adoption and Fostering 23*, 3, 6–15 and are reproduced with the permission of British Agencies for Adoption and Fostering (BAAF). The Index of Empathy has been reproduced with the permission of the author and the Society for Research in Child Development. The table of Kohlberg's stages of moral development has been reproduced from Schaffer, H. R. (1996) *Social Development* with the permission of Blackwell Publishers Inc.

I
Introduction to Resilience

Ecological framework

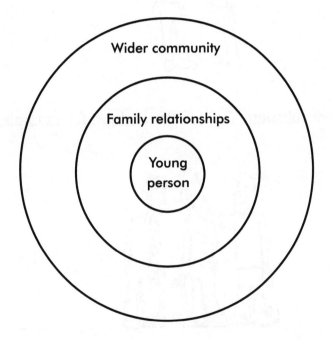

Figure 1.1 Three ecological levels at which resilience factors can be located

Throughout these workbooks the practitioner is encouraged to place assessment and intervention practice within an ecological framework (Bronfenbrenner 1989). This entails considering what resources might be available to the young person at each of three levels (see Figure 1.1):

1. the individual, for example, in dispositional and temperamental attributes

2. close family or substitute family relationships, for example, in secure attachments

3. the wider community, for example, in extrafamilial supports.

All the checklists will address aspects of each of these levels and suggestions for intervention will be provided for different ecological levels.

Resilience

Resilience can be defined as: 'Normal development under difficult conditions' (Fonagy *et al.* 1994).

Due to a wide range of practice and theoretical research, the protective factors that support positive outcomes, despite adversity, are becoming better understood (Rutter

1985; Werner 1990; Werner and Smith 1992). These protective factors that are associated with long-term social and emotional well-being have been located at all levels of the young person's ecological social environment. The existence of protective factors can help explain why one young person may cope better with adverse life events than another. The level of individual resilience can be seen as falling on a dimension of resilience and vulnerability (see Figure 1.2).

Figure 1.2 Dimension on which individual resilience can be located

This dimension is usually used to refer to intrinsic qualities of an individual. Some young people are more intrinsically resilient than others because of a whole range of factors that will be detailed later (Werner and Smith 1992). For example, an 'easy' temperament is associated with resilience in infancy.

A further dimension for the understanding of individual differences is that of protective and adverse environments; this dimension covers extrinsic factors and is therefore located at the outer ecological levels of family and wider community. Examples of protective factors are the existence of a close attachment and the presence of a supportive extended family member (see Figure 1.3).

Figure 1.3 Dimension on which factors of resilience around the young person can be located

When considered together these dimensions provide a framework for the assessment of adverse and positive factors at all ecological levels of a child's socio-emotional environment (Daniel, Wassell and Gilligan 1999) (see Figure 1.4).

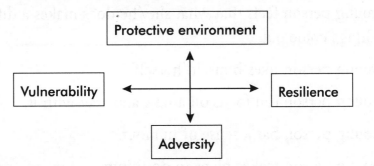

Figure 1.4 Framework for the assessment of resilience factors

The two dimensions will interact, an increase in protective factors will help to boost a child's individual resilience. Therefore, the workbook encourages the assessment of potential protective factors at each ecological level, with the aim of building up protective factors and thus boosting resilience.

Resilience is a complex issue and some caution is required. For example, it can be possible for young people to appear to be coping well with adversity, whereas in fact they may be internalising their symptoms (Luthar 1991). Apparent coping cannot be taken at face value and careful, wide-ranging assessment is essential.

The assessment of resilience is not straightforward: the vast majority of studies have been carried out retrospectively. However, a number of checklists have been devised that aim to measure levels of resilience. For example, the International Resilience Project uses a simple checklist of 15 items that indicate resilience in a young person (Grotberg 1997, p.20):

1. The young person has someone who loves him/her totally (unconditionally).

2. The young person has an older person outside the home she/he can tell about problems and feelings.

3. The young person is praised for doing things on his/her own.

4. The young person can count on her/his family being there when needed.

5. The young person knows someone he/she wants to be like.

6. The young person believes things will turn out all right.

7. The young person does endearing things that make people like her/him.

8. The young person believes in power greater than seen.

9. The young person is willing to try new things.

10. The young person likes to achieve in what he/she does.

11. The young person feels that what she/he does makes a difference in how things come out.

12. The young person likes himself/herself.

13. The young person can focus on a task and stay with it.

14. The young person has a sense of humour.

15. The young person makes plans to do things.

Although many factors can be associated with resilience, there appear to be three fundamental building blocks that underpin them (Gilligan 1997):

1. A secure base, whereby the young person feels a sense of belonging and security.

2. Good self-esteem, that is, an internal sense of worth and competence.

3. A sense of self-efficacy, that is, a sense of mastery and control, along with an accurate understanding of personal strengths and limitations.

These workbooks cover six domains of a child's life that will contribute to each of these three building blocks of resilience.

Because resilience is associated with better long-term outcomes, it can be used as a guiding principle when planning for young people whose lives have been disrupted by abuse and or neglect and who may require to be looked after away from home (Gilligan 1997). Indeed:

> Resilience – the capacity to transcend adversity – may be seen as the essential quality which care planning and provision should seek to stimulate as a key outcome of the care offered. (Gilligan 1997, p.14)

When the home life of a young person is disrupted for whatever reason, considerable attention is rightly paid to the issue of attachment and to placement, either in supporting the young person to live at home or in the provision of an appropriate alternative home life. However, whatever the arrangements for the day-to-day care of such young people, attention can also be paid to fostering their resilience. This approach recognises that although it may not always be possible to protect young people from further adversity, and that while it may not always be possible to provide an ideal environment for them, boosting their resilience should enhance the likelihood of a better long-term outcome.

A resilience-based approach focuses on maximising the likelihood of a better outcome for young people by building a protective network around them. The concept of resilience increasingly offers an alternative framework for intervention, the focus being on the assessment of potential areas of strength within the young person's whole system. As yet, there is very little research into proactive attempts to promote resilience.

Whatever arrangements are made for the care of the child, this approach offers social workers a real focus for positive practice. This approach enables a move away from an assumption that a parent or alternative placement will provide all that the young person needs. Instead the emphasis is on building a network of support from the resources available, and adding to them with professional support where necessary. It also emphasises the importance of building on the potential areas of resilience within the young person, for example, by maximising opportunities for engaging in hobbies, associating with friends, experiencing success, making a contribution and so on. What is important is that practitioners have the theoretical grounding that assures them that they can make a difference to the outcomes for children with such measures, even if they never see the results themselves. This assurance should help to reduce feelings of powerlessness and purposelessness.

DOMAINS OF RESILIENCE

Figure 1.5 Six domains of resilience

Throughout the workbooks aspects of resilience in six domains will be considered (see Figure 1.5).

Factors within each of these domains of a child's life, at each of the three ecological levels, are known to contribute to a child's level of vulnerability or resilience to adversity such as abuse, neglect and loss. More detail will be provided about each domain in the relevant section below.

It will be noted that these domains are similar to, but not identical with, the dimensions used in the Looking After Children (LAC) materials (Parker *et al.* 1991). However, much of the information required to assess resilience will be contained in completed LAC materials. The seven LAC dimensions can be linked with the six domains of resilience as follows:

1. Health: secure base

2. Education: education

3. Emotional and behavioural development: secure base/friendships/positive values

4. Family and peer relationships: secure base/friendships

5. Self-care and competence: secure base/social competencies

6. Identity: talents and interests

7. Social presentation: social competencies.

SUMMARY OF FACTORS ASSOCIATED WITH RESILIENCE DURING ADOLESCENT YEARS

Individual factors associated with resilience

- male
- responsibility
- empathy with others
- internal locus of control
- social maturity
- positive self-concept
- achievement orientation
- gentleness, nurturance
- social perceptiveness

- preference for structure
- a set of values
- intelligence
- willingness and capacity to plan.

Family factors associated with resilience

- close bond with at least one person
- nurturance and trust
- lack of separations
- lack of parental mental health or addiction problems
- required helpfulness
- encouragement for autonomy (girls)
- encouragement for expression of feelings (boys)
- close grandparents
- family harmony
- sibling attachment
- four or fewer children
- sufficient financial and material resources.

Wider community factors associated with resilience

- neighbour and other non-kin support
- peer contact
- good school experiences
- positive adult role models.

2

When and How to Use the Workbook

When?

These workbooks are intended as an aid to planning purposeful intervention with children and young people (see Figure 2.1). They are to be used in conjunction with Looking After Children materials when carrying out a comprehensive assessment of

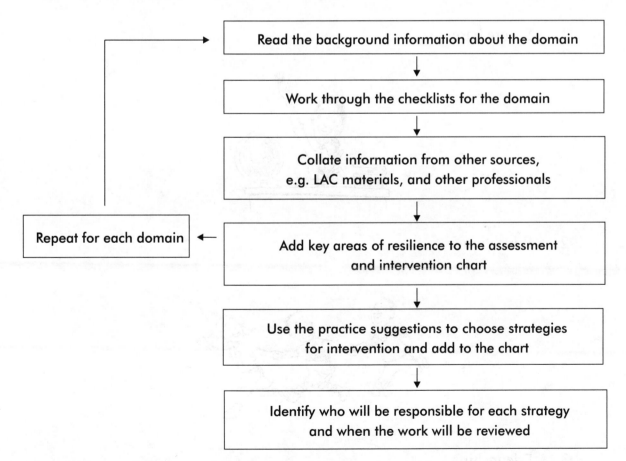

Figure 2.1 Process of assessment and planning for intervention

need; they can also be used to provide a baseline assessment against which the efficacy of intervention can be evaluated. They can be used to aid planning for children and young people living at home and for those living away from home.

How?

Ensure that you have chosen the appropriate workbook from one of three:

1. Pre-school children (early years)

2. School-age children

3. Adolescents.

The workbook takes you through a process of assessment for each of the six domains:

1. Secure base

2. Education

3. Friendships

4.   Talents and interests

5.   Positive values

6.   Social competencies.

Young person checklist

When using the young person's checklist try, as much as possible, to involve the young person directly in the process. Explain what you are trying to find out and cover each of the points in the checklists with the young person. Reword as appropriate. Try to arrange as much direct observation of behaviour as possible.

Parent/carer checklist

Go through the parent/carer checklist with any significant parent or carer. If there are significant differences between different people's responses, then explore this with the respondents and aim to reach a consensus on areas to work on.

A decision will need to be made for each situation as to whether to concentrate on an assessment of parental environment or carer environment. When the aim is for the young person to stay at or return home, the focus may need to be upon home environment. If the young person is to be accommodated on a long-term basis away from home, then the focus may need to be upon assessment of carer environment with a view to looking for aspects that might help with boosting resilience.

Use the checklists as a guide only, gather information from as wide range of sources as possible, particularly from the LAC materials, and try to involve the young person as much as possible, taking account of age and stage of development.

Assessment

Once you have assessed a domain, identify areas of actual or potential resilience at any ecological level that could be targeted for intervention and note them on the assessment and intervention chart. The assessment process is completed by bringing the information from each of the six domains together onto the chart.

Intervention

The workbook then takes you through a process of planning intervention. Look through the intervention strategies for each domain and use them to help plan strategies for the targeted areas for intervention. Note the strategies onto the assessment and intervention chart. In consultation with key people in the young person's life, identify who will be responsible for each strategy. Remember to consider the informal network as well as professionals.

Evaluation

Ensure that a plan for evaluation and ongoing monitoring is built into the strategy for intervention and note this onto the assessment and intervention chart.

Please remember:

1. One social worker cannot do it all. Aim to develop a network of formal and informal supports around the young person.

2. Look at existing, mainstream community resources.

3. Try to balance intervention that aims to build on existing strengths, with strategies for boosting less strong areas.

4. Positive effects in one domain can spill over to another, the domains should therefore not be viewed as independent and separate, but as interactive and dynamic.

Assessment and intervention chart

Domain	What areas of resilience, at any ecological level, will we target now?	How will we do this?	Who will be responsible for this?	How and when will we measure progress?
Secure base				
Education				

Friendships			
Talents and interests			
Positive values			
Social competencies			

Part I

Assessment

3

Secure Base

Background information

There is a clear association between the presence of a secure attachment relationship and resilience in the face of adversity (Werner 1990). The importance of attachment ties has been recognised in child-care practice for many years and normally underpins planning (Daniel *et al.* 1999; Fahlberg 1991; Howe 1995; Howe *et al.* 1999). It is during early years that the foundations of attachment are laid down. The classic studies to demonstrate attachment behaviour are normally carried out with toddlers, but elements of the behaviour can also be observed in older children (Ainsworth *et al.* 1978). These studies have shown that attachment behaviours can fall into one of several distinctive patterns. The most important distinction is between *secure* and *insecure* attachment. Young children who are classified as showing *secure* attachment play happily when their care-giver is present, protest when they leave and go to them for comfort on their return. They will show some wariness of strangers and choose their care-giver for comfort when upset or fearful. What they have is a base that not only is stable, but also acts as a springboard to the wider social world. Long-term resilience is associated with the opportunity to develop a secure attachment to at least one person.

Children who are classified as *insecure* may show one of four patterns.

1. If *avoidant* they tend to shun the care-giver after a separation and appear not to discriminate markedly in their behaviour towards a stranger and their care-giver.

2. If *ambivalent* they appear to want comfort from the care-giver after a separation, but at the same time show resistance to comfort, for example by squirming out of a hug.

3. A further form of insecure attachment, known as *disorganised*, is demonstrated in a mixture of reactions where the young person appears confused and unable to feel comforted by the care-giver. Young people who have been abused or neglected are more likely to show insecure patterns of attachment.

4. Another pattern of insecure attachment has been identified by Downes (1992) that is characterised by an *anxious preoccupation* with the availability of the carer. It is a pattern that can often be encountered in practice with abused and neglected children.

Adolescents may not show such overt signs of attachment, but their need for a secure base is as great as is the young child's. During adolescence the importance of the secure base as a springboard to the wider world is greater so that they can develop their own network of attachment relationships. During adolescence young people's close friendships are very important to them and they are also developing intimate, sexual relationships. Young people who are securely attached are more likely to be able to make the transition to mature interdependence with others.

Secure attachment is associated with a parenting style that is warm and sensitive. The parent has to be able to take account of the young person's needs and temperament and respond appropriately. Patterns of attachment are, therefore, the products of a *relationship* between the young person and the adult, and are influenced by the interaction between the young person (with his or her temperament) and the adult. The early pattern of attachment acts as a kind of template or internal working model for later relationships. The internal working model is, therefore, based upon the young person's sense of self and his or her experience of others. Howe *et al.* (1999, p.25) summarise it in the following way:

Self (loved, effective, autonomous and competent) + other people (available, cooperative and dependable) = *secure* attachment patterns.

Self (unloved but self-reliant) + other people (rejecting and intrusive) = *avoidant* attachment patterns.

Self (low value, ineffective and dependent) + other people (neglecting, insensitive, unpredictable and unreliable) = *ambivalent* attachment patterns.

Self (confused and bad) + other people (frightening and unavailable) = *disorganised* attachment patterns.

An important factor in the attachment relationship is the parent's own attachment history and the meaning it has for him or her. The way that adults talk about their own attachment experiences provides insight into their own level of security. Adults whose experience was of an abusive or neglectful childhood need not themselves be insecure. They can be considered secure if they have had an opportunity to process their experiences and can recount those experiences in a coherent way that suggests that they can make sense of their past (Main and Weston 1981). Having the opportunity and ability to reflect upon attachment experiences is key to overcoming difficult or disturbing past circumstances (Fonagy *et al.* 1994). It is also important to consider the ways in which current circumstances might undermine parents' ability to be sensitive to their child's needs, such as a difficult relationship with a partner, poverty, poor housing, social isolation and so on.

Young people may have a secure relationship with one person (for example, the father) and insecure with another (for example, the mother), therefore the quality of all important relationships must be assessed (Fox, Kimmerly and Schafer 1991). The aim in practice is to ensure that young people are provided with a secure base, either by improving the relationship with the parent/s or, if necessary, by finding an alternative attachment figure. Sometimes it can take a while to find long-term carers who will provide such secure relationships, but in the mean time there is tremendous potential for what Brooks (1994) describes as 'charismatic' adults to have a direct influence on a child's developing understanding of relationships. Insecure internal working models of attachment can change in the context of the formation of new, more secure relationships (Feeney and Noller 1996). During school years, and as they move into adolescence, young people will encounter a range of other adults, and among them may find someone that they can develop a relationship with. In practice, therefore, the aim would be to capitalise on the potential offered by any people, including absent fathers, siblings and extended family, family friends or professional staff, who take an interest in the young person (Gilligan 1999). Resilience theory would suggest an emphasis on building a protective network of support from all the resources available, and adding to them with professional support where necessary. During adolescence, young people may also value the opportunity to reflect upon their attachment experiences to date. If they can begin the process of being able to account for their own experiences in a coherent way then they are more likely to be able to become secure adults.

✓

SECURE BASE CHECKLIST
YOUNG PERSON

In a thorough and comprehensive text, Howe *et al.* (1999) set out detailed guidance for the assessment of patterns of attachment and the planning of intervention. If initial assessment suggests attachment problems to be the key issue then we would recommend that you consult this book for more information. They suggest that assessment must include making inquiries of the files and the wider professional network, observing children in various circumstances, and interviewing parents and children.

There needs to be a decision about which attachment relationships to assess. It is recommended that if the young person is living at home then an assessment be carried out on all significant adults, whether resident in the house or not, for example, mother, father, grandparent. If he or she is living away from home then the relationship with the carer or keyworker should be assessed, as well as any continuing family relationships. The following checklists should therefore be used flexibly and be adjusted according to requirements.

Does this young person appear to feel secure?

1. Observe the young person in a range of settings, at home and school. Look at how he or she deals with stress and distress, at how he or she relates to adults and other young people and at how willing the person is to explore the environment. From such observations it should be possible to build up a picture of the young person's general level of security. Teachers' views will be very helpful here, as they are, of course, able to observe the young person all day, in a range of situations.

Ask the young person:

1. Who do you think is the person in your life who most cares about you and loves you?

2. Who is important to you in your family?

3. What contact do you have with this person?

4. What do you think of

    (a) the frequency of contact with which you see them

    (b) the length of time you spend together

    (c) where this happens

    (d) the opportunities for doing things together?

5. How might this contact be improved?

6. Is there someone important you do not see that you would like to see?

7. When you say goodbye to someone you are close to, say, when you go to school or college, how does it make you feel?

8. Who is important in your life now?

9. Who do you see?

10. Who would you like to see?

11. Is there anything that you would like to change about who you see?

12. Can you describe any separations or losses that you remember happening?

13. How confident do you feel about making new relationships with other young people and with other adults?

Does the current parent or carer environment provide the young person with a secure base?

1. Observe the interaction between the young person and each significant adult. Use the observations of the verbal and non-verbal aspects of the relationship and the consistency and sensitivity of the adult's response to the young person to gauge the quality of the attachment relationship.

2. Is there predictability of care?

3. Observe the young person at times of separation from and reunion with significant adults. Does the young person show a healthy pattern of separation or are there signs of over-anxiety, clinginess or indifference?

✓

Ask the young person:

1. If you are upset about something, how do you show what you feel and who would you turn to?

2. Do you feel that your parent or carer is able to make time for you?

3. (If the young person is living away from home) do you have contact with a parent and do you know why you have that contact?

What are the wider resources that contribute to the young person's attachment network?

In collaboration draw an ecomap using circles to represent the young person and any other person who is, or who has been, important to the young person, including other young people. Map the young person's network, with the person who is most important to the young person closest to him or her. A series of ecomaps can be used to represent the past, the present and what the young person would like for the future.

Ask the young person:

1. How do you feel about the relationships you have with important adults in your life?

2. In situations of marital separation how are the arrangements made for contact with your non-custodial parent and extended family, or if accommodated with both sides of the family?

3. Is there any other family member who can offer support to you?

4. What is the nature and level of contact with siblings who are

    (a) at home

    (b) away in independent living arrangements

    (c) away from home in other placements?

5. Do you have unresolved feelings about particular relationships from the past?

6. Who can you talk to about these relationships?

Adolescence, © Brigid Daniel and Sally Wassell 2002 © Iain Campbell 2002

7. Who might be some of the key people you will need for support once you leave local authority accommodation or once you leave home and how might contact with these important people be made possible well before this stage?

8. Do you attend any clubs or activities run by adults that you like and trust? If not, would you like to attend something like this?

✓

SECURE BASE CHECKLIST
PARENT/CARER

Does this young person appear to feel secure?

Ask the parent/carer:

1. Who is important to this young person?

2. How does the young person demonstrate the importance of the relationship?

3. What contact does he or she have with these people?

4. How do you consult with the young person about his or her changing wishes and feelings about contact?

5. Is there someone the young person has not seen for some time who may be important?

6. What does he or she do if upset? How does he or she show their distress and show that they want comfort?

7. How willing is he or she to explore new places, activities and so on?

8. Does he or she react differently to unknown adults from how he or she reacts to known adults?

9. What significant losses or separations has this young person experienced?

Does the current parent or carer environment provide the young person with a secure base?

1. Ask the parent about his or her own experiences of loss, separation and rejection, experiences of emotional upsets, hurts and sickness and his or her experiences of love and acceptance with their parents or carers. Consider the nature of the account. Is he or she able to provide a clear, coherent and considered description of his or her own experiences? Does it appear that he or

she would benefit from an opportunity to reflect upon his or her attachment history?

2. Use the quality of attachment measure (devised by Lucy Berliner and David Fine). It can be used to help assess the attachment pattern.

Ask the parent/carer:

1. What do you think the relationship between you and the young person is like? Is it as you would like it to be, or are there aspects that worry you? (If it may be of help, describe the different patterns of attachment to the parent.)

2. What is your routine of care? (For example, mealtimes, times for the young person to be in at night etc.)

3. What happens when you and the young person separate? Does he or she show signs of over-anxiety, clinginess or indifference?

4. What do you usually do to comfort the young person when he or she is distressed? Does this usually work?

5. Do you find that you can make time for the young person?

6. (If the young person is living away from home) do you feel that you have enough contact with the young person? What do you understand the reason for the contact to be?

What are the wider resources that contribute to the young person's attachment network?

Ask the parent/carer:

1. Could you name all the people (adult or young person) that the young person knows, or has known in the past, who you think are important to him or her?

2. Do you feel that you have enough support to be able to be a good parent? Is there anything that you think makes it difficult to parent, for example, lack of money, poor housing, lack of friends, lack of educational opportunities and so on?

3. Can you think of anybody that you know who may be able to spend some time with the young person?

4. If the young person does not attend any clubs or activities, do you think this would be of benefit?

✓

QUALITY OF ATTACHMENT

This tool has been developed by Lucy Berliner and David Fine, Center for Sexual Assault and Traumatic Stress, Harborview Medical Center, Seattle, Washington and is reproduced with their permission. The process of detailed evaluation and validation of this material is currently underway. Modified versions may therefore be produced in the future.

Four short descriptions are provided which relate to each of the four types of attachment:

- secure attachment (Type B)

- insecure – avoidant (Type A)

- insecure – ambivalent (Type C)

- insecure – disorganised (Type D)

Simply ask the parent or carer to say which description best fits the young person's attachment behaviour.

Child/adolescent smiles, and often seeks physical contact when greeting you; having you present relaxes child; s/he is usually comfortable when alone or separated from you. (B)

Child/adolescent appears independent, almost too independent for their age; s/he may avoid you; s/he is not upset at separation; child/adolescent is as comfortable with strangers as family members. (A)

Child/adolescent is clingy and anxious with you; gets upset when separated from you and may have difficulty being alone; s/he is glad to see you, but at the same time may act angry or upset. (C)

Child/adolescent may show a mixture of being distant and anxious; s/he can be angry and controlling or be compliant, but in an overly sweet/fake way. (D)

4

Education

Background information

Good educational attainment is associated with good outcomes and is therefore a protective factor that should be aimed for (Rutter 1991). School or college also offer a wide range of other opportunities to boost resilience, including acting as a complementary secure base, providing many opportunities for developing self-esteem and efficacy and opportunities for constructive contact with peers and supportive adults (Garbarino *et al.* 1992; Gilligan 1998).

It is now recognised that being accommodated away from home is likely to have a significant negative impact upon educational achievement (Jackson 1995; Parker *et al.* 1991). Government policy initiatives are aimed at this problem (Scottish Office 1999). When young people are accommodated away from home the focus of intervention during adolescence is often upon planning for moving on from local authority accommodation. Issues of education can be pushed to the background, especially if the young person has not been attending school for some time. However, there are such clear associations between early school leaving, lack of qualifications and poor long-term outcomes that it essential that the issue of education be kept as a priority throughout planning (Rutter 1991).

Although considerable strides in cognitive development occur during middle school years, cognitive processes continue to mature during adolescence. Through teenage years and into early adulthood, young people may move into the stage known as formal operations when the ability to grasp abstract concepts increases, when hypothetical reasoning becomes possible and logic is more sophisticated (Piaget 1952). Such cognitive skills are more likely to develop if the young person is intellectually stimulated and spends time in an educational setting. If a young person reaches adolescence unable to read, this must be taken seriously. Literacy is known to be valued especially highly by young people who have experienced adversity and who have been accommodated by the local authority (Jackson 1995). Many young people who have 'succeeded from care' have discovered the pleasures of reading.

As young people begin to approach adulthood, there may be a process of taking stock. A major issue for many adolescents is the notion that their own subculture dictates that learning is definitely not cool. This means that parents and carers have to be skilful in capturing, nurturing and harnessing the young person's imagination, interest and creativity in ways that connect directly with the young person's aims for life after school. It is often not sufficient to extol the benefits of learning in themselves as young people who have experienced many interruptions to their learning have usually lost confidence in their capacity to make progress. If at this stage they can appreciate the importance of qualifications for future choices they may be willing to reconsider their attitudes to learning. As we know, a sense of self-efficacy is a foundation of resilience and if the young person can be encouraged to believe that he or she can make a choice about continuing education in some form feelings of self-efficacy are likely to be enhanced. The benefit of moving into adolescence and young adulthood is that the choices of the site of learning widen. For example, many young people find a college setting much more appealing than school.

Some young people see school as a haven and make good progress. In fact the whole area of schooling, or even one subject in particular, may constitute an 'island of competence' in an otherwise bleak set of circumstances (Brookes 1994). Many neglected children have not had the opportunity to explore their abilities, particularly if they were also undermined emotionally, criticised or ignored. Therefore, finding the area of ability in learning may be a testing task. Often carers will happen upon a skill that has been hidden. A young person's enthusiasm outside of school can deliberately be linked with learning tasks within the school setting. For example, learning to prepare the necessary arrangements for an enjoyable activity, for example, a musical festival, where preparing for a trip can include the necessary practical tasks and strategies for problem solving and negotiation with peers. All of these elements are learning points and the young person will often see the force of these more readily than in an apparently artificial school exercise.

Because of low self-esteem, disruptive behaviour in a young person who has experienced adversity often leads to a difficulty in taking an initiative in school in a positive way. Some young people may well refuse to cooperate simply to make their mark by evading challenges or confronting adults and or peers. It can be an idea to turn the tables deliberately by giving young people extra responsibility for a particular task as long as the conditions are such that they will be supported. This can have surprising results.

Successful educational experiences are fostered by good support for learning from parents and/or carers. Some young people will need extra help in learning because of early gaps or interruptions in their learning or overall development. As with younger children, the *supportive relationships* available to them may often be a critical factor in increased progress. Gearing the expectations of them to high but reasonable standards requires real attention to the adolescent and a detailed awareness of their ability and needs. Harnessing the young person's natural curiosity and enthusiasm is also a vehicle for encouraging social development in the older teenager. When assessing who has the potential to offer educational support, parents and other family members can be considered, even if young people do not live with them. Such a person could be a volunteer, mentor from the community, family member, keyworker in a residential unit, or the like.

It can be helpful to consider three different aspects of education:

- the school or college as a place

- education as a process

- educators as people.

Each of these aspects is important and it may be helpful to look at whether there are strengths or problems in each. For example, as a place school or college can, for some, be a haven of regularity and safety while for others it may be the site of bullying. For young people with poor social skills, interaction with other young people may be a source of stress and anxiety and may interfere with learning. For others it may be a source of friendship. For some young people the process of learning is fun and challenging, for others it can seem threatening and frightening. Finally, the school or college staff form a pool of concerned adults among whom the young person can find someone who is a source of emotional and/or intellectual support.

✓

EDUCATION CHECKLIST
YOUNG PERSON

First, it is necessary to have an up-to-date educational assessment and to identify any particular areas where extra support is needed. This assessment must be carried out by education staff and, where appropriate, an educational psychologist. Close cooperation with education staff is essential both during assessment and when planning and carrying out an intervention package. If the young person is not attending school some of the questions will need to refer to previous experiences of school.

To what extent does the young person show an interest in school, college and learning?

Ask the young person:

1. Why do you think young people have to go to school?

2. What do (or did) you think of your school? (If he or she has been to different schools ask how they compare, what did he or she like about each.)

3. If you could change something in your school, what would it be?

4. How do (or did) you feel when you go into the school building?

5. Do you find that you can concentrate in class? If not, why not?

6. What is your favourite subject or what do you enjoy learning about?

7. Who would you go to if you did not understand something in your favourite subject?

8. Who would you ask for help in your least favourite subject?

9. What would you most like to learn about next?

10. Do you think there is anything that you need extra help with, for example, reading?

11. What would you most like to achieve this term?

12. If you are not attending school at the moment what do you think would be the best way for you to continue your education (for example, at college, a job in combination with college, evening classes, tutoring)?

13. How do you get on with the other young people at school (or college)?

To what extent does the parent or carer environment facilitate the young person's learning and school or college attendance?

Ask the young person:

1. Who knows what you are doing at school or college? If you are not attending any education establishment is anyone encouraging you and helping you back to education?

2. Who do you think takes an interest in your school or college progress?

3. How much do your parents and/or carers know about your school or college progress?

4. Do you have a private place to study?

5. Who helps you with your homework?

6. Who goes to school or college meetings and who would you like to go to school meetings?

What opportunities are there in the wider environment to support this young person's education?

Ask the young person:

1. Do you meet up with any of the young people you know at school or college at other times? If not, would you like to be able to meet up with anyone more?

2. Is (or was) there any teacher in particular (or member of support staff) who you find easy to talk to and who helps you with school issues?

3. Is there anyone else that you know outside school or college who can help you with your studying (for example an aunt or uncle, grandparent or friend)?

4. Do you go to any learning clubs, such as a computer club, and if you don't do you think something like that could be helpful?

✓

EDUCATION CHECKLIST
PARENT/CARER

To what extent does the young person show an interest in school, college and learning?

Ask the parent/carer:

1. Do you have an accurate assessment of the young person's current level of achievement? If not, who can help you with this from the school or college setting? Are you kept informed about the young person's performance?

2. Do you think he or she understands the purpose of education?

3. How would you describe his or her experience of school, for example, positive, extremely variable, reluctant, avoidant, completely resistant?

4. What is the young person's attitude to learning?

5. Do you think that he or she has a sense of belonging in school or college now or has had in the past?

6. Do you think that he or she is able to concentrate on their studies?

7. What are the *young person's* interests? Have these interests been linked with the young person's time at school or college? If not, how might this be done?

8. What is this young person good at?

9. If this young person is described as slow or interrupted or delayed, what does this mean to you from your knowledge of the young person? Do you think there is anything that he or she needs extra help with, for example, reading?

10. What would you most like the young person to achieve this term?

11. If he or she is not attending school at the moment what do you think would be the best way for him or her to continue their education (for example, at college, a job in combination with college, evening classes, tutoring)?

12. How do you think that he or she gets on with the other young people at school?

To what extent does the parent or carer environment facilitate the young person's learning and school or college attendance?

Ask the parent/carer:

1. Who knows what the young person is doing at school? Who tracks whether work is completed and to a satisfactory standard? If he or she is not attending any education establishment is anyone encouraging them and helping them back to education?

2. Who can/is helping you to set out activities, help and ideas focused on what he or she needs to learn next?

3. Who helps you with strategies for helping the young person to learn? How are these strategies reviewed?

4. Does he or she have a private place to study?

5. Who helps with studies?

6. Who attends school or college meetings? If you don't, would you like to be able to?

7. When was this young person's last success at school or college? How was this marked or celebrated and by whom, at home and/or at school or college?

8. What were your own experiences of school?

9. Would you like access to educational opportunities yourself?

✓

What opportunities are there in the wider environment to support this young person's education?

Ask the parent/carer:

1. Does he or she meet up with any young people from school or college at other times? If not, are there ways that this could be encouraged and supported?

2. Is there any teacher in particular (or member of support staff) that the young person appears to have (or have had) a good relationship with?

3. Is there anyone in the community who could act as a mentor in relation to his or her learning? Who could help them now by offering time and high, but reasonable, expectations of achievement?

4. Does he or she attend any learning clubs (for example, a computer club), and if not do you think something like that could be helpful?

5

Friendships

Background information

> From a remarkably early age, children not only can describe their various network associates, but can offer candid appraisals of the extent of support they expect from each. (Thompson 1995, p.34)

Resilience is associated with having generally positive peer relationships, and, specifically, good friendships (Werner 1990). Much research has been carried out about the importance of social support for adults and more is emerging about the importance of such social support for young people. It is known that having friends can help buffer the effects of stress, prevent stress, mediate stress and provide information to deal with stress. The key issue for adults appears to be the perception of having support (Thompson 1995). The issues for young people are similar, but there are unique features of their friendships due to developmental stage, autonomy and power. Friendships in childhood allow for horizontal (equal) relationships, which complement the vertical relationships they have with adults. This allows them to learn the social skills of interacting with equals, such as competition and cooperation and in this way young people socialise each other (Schaffer 1996). As well as offering opportunities for fun and companionship, Hartup (1992) describes friendships as providing:

- contexts in which to acquire or elaborate social skills
- self-knowledge and knowledge about others
- emotional support in times of stress
- the basis for future intimate relationships.

Conversely, the lack of friends during childhood is associated with a range of problems (Schaffer 1996):

- emotional problems

- immature perspective-taking ability

- less altruism

- poor social skills in group entry, cooperative play and conflict management

- less sociability

- poor school adjustment

- poorer school attainment.

There is likely to be a circular pattern whereby young people who already show problems such as aggressiveness and poor social skills have difficulty in making friends and are therefore less likely to have the opportunity to learn better skills.

Although good peer relationships can compensate to some extent for poor attachment experiences, there is evidence of an association between the quality of attachments and the quality of friendships. Young people with secure attachments tend to relate to peers in a positive and responsive way, whereas young people with insecure avoidant attachments may show either aggression towards or detachment from peers (Howe 1995). Social support can buffer the effects of adversity, but maltreatment can impair peer relationships so that those who need social support the most are the least likely to have it (Thompson 1995). In their study of young people leaving care, Biehal *et al.* found that those who had poor friendship networks also tended to have poor relationships with parents, while those who had good relationships with parents had good networks of friends. There was also an association between having good relationships (both family and wider) and a positive sense of identity, which was in turn associated with good self-esteem.

Triseliotis *et al.* (1995) found that, in spite of disruptive experiences, most of the 13–17-year-old young people in receipt of social work intervention that were interviewed identified friends as playing an important part in their lives. But they also found that social workers were often not well informed about teenagers' social networks. In her study of a number of leaving care schemes Stone (1989, p.56) showed that there 'was no instance of young people building up or fitting into anything like a community network'. This suggests that social workers need to pay particular attention to young people's friendships when they move to independence.

In early school years friendship is normally based on proximity and the peer network is highly dependent upon parents and carers. School greatly widens children's networks and as children get older they make more active efforts to develop a network that is built upon common interests (Smith and Cowie 1991).

When children move into adolescence the strict gender divide in activities seen in middle school years starts to break down (Golombok and Fivush 1994). There may be large same-sex cliques or gangs but also a move towards heterosexual couples, and a number will choose homosexual relationships. There is a real change in the character of friendships as they become much more intimate. The number of best friends a young person identifies might decrease from the average of seven during middle school years, but the best friendships become more intense and involve the sharing of private thoughts, especially among girls (Schaffer 1996). Adolescents describe friends in terms of loyalty, commitment, genuineness and intimacy (Bigelow and La Gaipa 1980). Friends are seen as people who boost your sense of self-worth.

Younger children's networks tend to be mediated by parents and carers, but during adolescence complex peer relationships that are independent of the family become very important. In summary, friendships in adolescence are (Thompson 1995):

- more extensive

- more exclusive (involving intimacy and loyalty)

- more multidimensional (mix of friendships and sexually intimate relationships)

- important for reducing stress, mediating stress and preventing stress.

Being able to make friends is only part of the equation; the type of friendships made is another. Not having friends can be associated with a range of problems, but having antisocial friends can also be unhelpful. Triseliotis *et al.* (1995) found that 60 per cent of the young people interviewed said that a friend had got them into trouble at some point. Young people who have experienced sexual abuse are more likely to go on to have psychiatric problems by 18 if their friendships are with substance abusing or delinquent peers (Lynskey and Fergusson 1997). From a study of a range of problems such as alcohol and substance misuse, truanting and law-breaking in 940 teenagers, Fergusson and Lynskey (1996) concluded:

Resilient teenagers were characterised as adolescents having fewer affiliations with delinquent peers assessed by both parental and self report. There were, however, no significant differences between the two groups in terms of their level of peer attachments. (Fergusson and Lynskey 1996, pp.287–288)

Similarly Bender and Lösel (1997) state:

Being a member of a peer group correlates with greater satisfaction with social support. Although this looks like a positive social resource and may be protective against internalizing symptoms, the effect on antisocial behaviour is partially negative: neither boys nor girls changed their degree of problem behaviour when they felt integrated in a peer group and well supported. This is in line with research showing that adolescents select companions who are similar to themselves. (Bender and Lösel 1997, p.672)

So, if young people are already showing antisocial behaviour there is a strong likelihood that they will mix with others who show antisocial behaviour and that friendships will reinforce their behaviour. On the other hand, less antisocial young people are protected by having friendships.

FRIENDSHIPS CHECKLIST
YOUNG PERSON

What characteristics does this young person have that help with making and keeping friends?

1. Either give the checklist 'My friends and me as a friend' that follows to the young person to fill in, or go through it with him or her. If this does not seem appropriate, or does not provide enough information, you could try the following.

2. Have a general chat with the young person about how he or she gets on with other young people, for example, simple scenarios can be used to see how they enter a group. For example, 'Coming out of school/college you run into a group of people you like who are about to go into town and you would like to go along with them. What would you say or do, and what would be likely to happen?'

3. At this age it should be possible to find out who the young person thinks of as friends by simply asking: 'Who are your friends?' and 'Who are your best friends?' If he or she has difficulty with this you could use some of the methods described in the *School Years* workbook.

4. Ask the young person to tell you what he or she thinks a friend is. If the young person cannot come up with an answer give some choices, such as 'someone you hang around with', 'someone who lives nearby', 'someone to have fun with', 'someone who likes the same things as you do', 'someone to help you if you have problems', 'someone you can trust', 'someone you can tell your private thoughts to' and so on.

✓

To what extent does the parent or carer environment facilitate the development of friendship?

Ask the young person:

1. Do any of your friends ever spend time at your house?

2. Have you got any friends that are not through school, but are the children of your parent's friends or are cousins?

3. If you want to meet up with a friend, would your parent or carer help you, for example by making the arrangements, taking you to his or her house, and so on?

4. Is your parent or carer ever there when you are with friends, and if they are what do they do if an argument breaks out?

What are the young person's friendships like at the moment?

From your observations and despite their own report, does the young person appear to have any particular friends?

Ask the young person:

1. Have your friends ever got you into trouble?

2. Do you ever feel pushed or bullied into doing something you don't want to by your friends?

3. Are you ever scared about the things that your friends do?

4. Do you think that adults don't approve of your friends?

5. What opportunities are there for you to have contact with young people other than at school, for example, are there local youth clubs or groups you can join or have joined?

MY FRIENDS AND ME AS A FRIEND

You can write whatever you like in answer to each question. If you are not sure of what to put, just write that you aren't sure.

1.   If you hear the word 'friend', what does it mean to you?

2.   Why do you think people like to have friends?

3.   What things about you would make people want to be your friend?

4.   How many friends do you have?

5.   How many of your friends are *best* friends?

6.   What do you like about your friends?

7.   Do you see your friends as much as you would like to?

8.   Do you ever worry that you don't get on very well with other children?

9.   What sort of things do you like to do with your friends?

✓

10. Are there any friends that you have not seen for ages, but would like to?

11. Do you ever find that other children won't let you join in their games?

12. Have any of your friends ever got you into trouble?

13. Do you have a friend that you can talk to about things that worry you?

14. Are you happy with the way things are with your friends, or is there anything that you would like to be different?

15. Who would you talk to about any problems that you have with any of your friends?

FRIENDSHIPS CHECKLIST
PARENT/CARER

What characteristics does this young person have that help with making and keeping friends?

Ask the parent/carer:

1. How does this young person get on with other young people? Does he or she seem a lot shyer than other young people, or a lot more pushy, or does he or she get on well with others?

2. If we ask the young person 'Who are your best friends?' what do you think he or she will say?

3. If we ask the young person 'What is a friend?' what do you think he or she will say?

To what extent does the parent or carer environment facilitate the development of friendship?

Ask the parent/carer:

1. Do any of the young person's friends ever spend time at their house?

2. Have any of the young person's friends been made through you, for example with young people of your friends or family?

3. How much would you get involved in any arrangements the young person might make to see friends?

4. Do you get much chance to see how the young person gets on with other young people? If so, how would you intervene if you saw them falling out?

✓

What are the young person's friendships like at the moment?

Ask the parent/carer:

1. Sometimes young people describe another young person as a friend or best friend, but in fact the other young person probably wouldn't see him or her as a friend. Would this be the case for this young person, or does he or she seem to have at least one good friend?

2. Are you ever worried that the friends he or she has are a bad influence?

3. Do you find yourself worrying that the young person is easily led?

4. What opportunities are there for the young person to have contact with young people other than at school, for example, are there local youth clubs or groups he or she can join or has joined?

Adolescence, © Brigid Daniel and Sally Wassell 2002 © Iain Campbell 2002

6

Talents and Interests

Background information

Self-esteem is one of the fundamental building blocks of resilience. Self-esteem has been defined as: 'Appreciating my own worth and importance and having the character to be accountable for myself and to act responsibly toward others' (California State Department of Education, cited in Brooks 1994, p.547).

This definition highlights the importance of the interpersonal element of self-esteem. Having a healthy sense of self-esteem is not just about feeling good about oneself while having no regard for the impact of oneself upon others. Therefore, the goal of much long-term work with young people is not only to help them to feel better about themselves, but also to help them recognise the importance of interrelationships and of empathy with others. Self-esteem appears to be linked with levels of self-efficacy which is also known to be associated with resilience and which is discussed in more detail in the Social Competence domain (Luthar 1991). So, young people with high self-esteem have a realistic notion of their abilities and see successes as due to their own efforts and within their control. Those with low esteem are more likely to attribute any successes to chance. They see failures as due to unchangeable factors, for example a lack of ability or intelligence. They demonstrate a sense of helplessness and hopelessness, expect to fail and show self-defeating behaviour (Brooks 1994).

Harter (1985) suggests that self-esteem is based in the balance between what young people would like to be and what they think they actually are. Everyone has an 'ideal' self and a 'perceived' self, and the closer they are to each other, the healthier the self-esteem. Self-esteem is not simply related to being good at something. A young person may be very good at mathematics, but not value that skill. Also, a young person who would like to be good at art, but perceives that his or her drawings are poor, will have a lower esteem than a young person who does not value art and whose drawings are poor.

In her studies of self-esteem, Harter (1985) looked at a global measure of self-esteem (general self-worth) as well as eight separate domains for adolescents:

- scholastic competence

- athletic competence

- social acceptance

- physical appearance

- behavioural conduct

- close friendship

- romantic appeal

- job competence.

Harter found the different domains to be independent of each other, so for example, a young person might have a high score in one area and a low one in another. It is not until young people reach the age of about 6 or 7 that a reliable, separate global rating of self-esteem can be measured. So, younger people's self-esteem can fluctuate and vary according to circumstances (Harter 1985). Self-esteem can change and is amenable to improvement. During the school years the potential for boosting self-esteem, especially through activities at school, is great. Adolescence is not necessarily a time when problems with self-esteem can occur, if at all it is girls who are most likely to feel a drop in self-esteem, especially in the domain of physical appearance, but global self-esteem may not be affected, or may even rise.

The roots of esteem lie firmly in early attachment experiences and enduring feelings based on early experiences of being loved. Studies of 10–11-year-old boys have shown high self-esteem to be associated with parents who have high self-esteem themselves and who are very accepting of their young people and allow them freedom, but within clearly defined and enforced limits. Low self-esteem is associated with rejection and either authoritarian or permissive parenting (Coopersmith 1997). Self-esteem is also affected by relationships with classmates, friends and teachers (Harter 1985).

A study of outcomes for teenagers subject to social service intervention showed an association between good outcomes and pre-intervention high self-esteem and good school progress (Triseliotis *et al.* 1995).

Therefore, encouraging the young person's unique talents and interests can help to boost resilience. If a young person has a natural talent it should be nurtured, and, more importantly, the young person should learn to value that talent. If a young person has an interest, that interest should be supported, even if the young person has no special talent in the area. Many young people who have experienced adversity and who may be either at home or 'looked after' may have hidden attributes and potential that have not emerged under conditions of stress and confusion. For example, young people who are preoccupied with surviving abuse, or living with domestic violence, may have learned to use their energies in adapting to complex or changing family circumstances, and hence will not have had the chance or energy to make use of available opportunities. Those young people who adapt to stress and trauma by becoming passive, or those with particularly low self-esteem, may have little or no sense of their own particular aptitudes. The challenge for practitioners is therefore to find ways of creating opportunities for young people to experience feelings of success, perhaps by looking for 'islands of competence' (Brooks 1994).

Remarkably, some young people still demonstrate unusual capacities and abilities, even in the most stressful circumstances and here the *continuity* of opportunity through any necessary changes or transitions will be of real importance. For example, the young person who shows skill in physical coordination, who has enjoyed gymnastics and yet has to leave home or move to another placement, will benefit from continuing with the activity if at all possible.

✓

TALENTS AND INTERESTS CHECKLIST
YOUNG PERSON

What talents does this young person have and does he or she have any particular interests?

Remember that what the young person is interested in, what he or she values and what he or she is good at might all be different. The value he or she places on a skill might also be influenced by peer and social pressure, particularly if it is not one socially associated with their gender (for example, a boy interested in dance).

1. Use the list of activities and hobbies that follows 'What can I do and what would I like to do?' to help identify areas of interest value and skill. It may also be helpful to use magazines and catalogues to trigger ideas.

2. A scale for self-esteem also follows that can be used with young people to help determine how good they feel about themselves.

Ask the young person:

1. What hobbies, activities and other things are you interested in?

2. Is there anything that any of your friends do that you wish you could try?

3. What things that you do at the moment do you enjoy?

4. Are there things that you think you are pretty good at?

5. Are there things that you wish you were good at?

6. Are there any activities that you would like to try?

7. Is there anything that you used to do or be good at that you would like to try again?

Does the parent or carer environment encourage the development and expression of talents and interests?

Ask the young person:

1. Is anyone in your family interested in the same things as you?

2. Does anyone in your family have a hobby that you share or that you would like to share?

3. Do you feel that your parents or carers help you to keep up with your interests (e.g. give you fees, take you to meetings etc.)?

4. How interested do you think your parent or carer is in the things you do?

What opportunities are there in the wider environment for the nurturing of this young person's talents and interests?

Ask the young person:

1. Can you think of anyone you know who might help you do something you are interested in, for example, grandparent, older sibling, uncle or aunt, friend's parent and so on?

2. Do you know of local hobby clubs or groups near where you live that you do, or would like to, attend?

3. Are there any clubs or activities at your school or college that you do, or would like to, attend?

4. Is there anyone else that you think could help you with your hobbies, for example, keyworker, teacher, social worker?

✓

WHAT CAN I DO AND WHAT WOULD I LIKE TO DO?

Activity	Am pretty good at	Would like to try
sports		
art		
drama		
music		
martial arts		
dance		
gymnastics		
computing		
crafts		
modelling		
creative writing		
photography		
swimming		
fishing		
chess		
keeping pets/animals		
horse-riding		
keep-fit		
Scouts, Brownies or Guides, Boys'/Girls' Brigade, Woodcraft		
cycling		
skating/skateboarding/scooting		
hill walking		
cookery		
collecting		
skiing		
sailing		

Adolescence, © Brigid Daniel and Sally Wassell 2002 © Iain Campbell 2002

SELF-ESTEEM

The Rosenberg Self Esteem Scale is in the public domain and can be copied.

Please read each statement. Then circle the letter indicating how much you agree or disagree with the statement.

	Strongly agree	Agree	Disagree	Strongly disagree
1. I feel that I am a person of worth. I am as good as anybody else.	A	B	C	D
2. I feel that there are a lot of good things about me.	A	B	C	D
3. I feel that I fail a lot.	A	B	C	D
4. I can do things as well as most other people.	A	B	C	D
5. I do not have much to be proud of.	A	B	C	D
6. I wish I had more respect for myself.	A	B	C	D
7. I feel useless at times.	A	B	C	D
8. Sometimes I think I am no good at all.	A	B	C	D
9. I like myself.	A	B	C	D
10. I am happy with myself.	A	B	C	D

✓

Scoring for Rosenberg Self Esteem Scale

For questions 3, 5, 6, 7 and 8 apply the following points:

    A 1

    B 2

    C 3

    D 4

For questions 1, 2, 4, 9 and 10 apply the following points:

    A 4

    B 3

    C 2

    D 1

Add up the total number of points and divide by the number of questions to give the final score. The higher the score the higher the level of self-esteem.

Adolescence, © Brigid Daniel and Sally Wassell 2002 © Iain Campbell 2002

TALENTS AND INTERESTS CHECKLIST
PARENT/CARER

What talents does this young person have and does he or she have any particular interests?

Explain to the parent or carer that what the young person is interested in, what he or she values and what he or she is good at might all be different and that you want to find out about all areas.

Ask the parent/carer:

1. What hobbies, activities and other things is the young person interested in?

2. Can you think of any activities that the young person seems to enjoy?

3. Does the young person show signs of having a particular skill or talent, for example, in art, sport and so on? If so, does he or she value that skill?

4. Do you know what activities and skills that the young person thinks it is important to be good at?

5. Do you think there are any other activities that the young person might enjoy trying?

6. Can you think of anything that the young person used to show signs of being good at in the past that could be picked up on again?

7. How good do you think he or she feels about him or herself?

✓

Does the parent or carer environment encourage the development and expression of talents and interests?

Ask the parent/carer:

1. Are there activities that you enjoy, do you have time to take part in them, and could they be shared with the young person?

2. Does anyone in your family have a hobby that the young person does, or could share?

3. Do you find that you are able to help the young person take part in activities? If not, what gets in the way, for example, lack of time, money or energy?

What opportunities are there in the wider environment for the nurturing of this young person's talents and interests?

Ask the parent/carer:

1. Can you think of anyone you know who might help the young person do something he or she is interested in, for example, grandparent, older sibling, uncle or aunt, friends and so on?

2. Do you know of local hobby clubs or groups near where you live that the young person does, or would like to attend? If not, would you like help finding out this information?

3. Do you know of any clubs or activities at the school or college that he or she does, or would like to attend? Would you like more information about this?

4. Is there anyone else that you think could help with hobbies and activities, for example, keyworker, teacher, social worker?

7

Positive Values

Background information

Holding positive values and having the capacity to act in a helpful, caring and responsible way towards others is associated with resilience (Benson 1997; Raundalen 1991; Werner and Smith 1992). Such 'prosocial' behaviour is displayed in actions towards others that are not based on the expectation of external rewards (Smith and Cowie 1991) and include:

- helping others
- comforting others in distress
- sharing with others.

As they enter adolescence, young people should already be able to demonstrate fairly mature moral reasoning. They should have an understanding of the importance of intention, and be able to distinguish between accidental harm and intentional harm to another person or to property. They should be able to take another person's perspective and realise that different people may have different values. They should understand about mutual expectations of behaviour and of the need to live up to what significant others expect of them. They will also develop a greater grasp of principles such as trust and loyalty and abstract notions such as justice. This is known as the 'conventional' stage of moral reasoning, and is the stage that many people attain (Kohlberg 1969). Some, but by no means all, adolescents will move into the 'postconventional' level in which universal human principles are sometimes set above laws (see Appendix for more details about moral reasoning).

A young person may be able to articulate what is 'right' and 'wrong', but may still do what is 'wrong'. However, because there does tend to be an association between young people's level of moral reasoning and their moral behaviour, especially delinquency and aggression (Eisenberg *et al.* 1991; Goldstein 1999) it is important that it be taken into account when assessing elements of positive values. So, for example, adolescents involved in aggressive behaviour and delinquency may reason at the preconventional stage. They might say it is all right to steal if someone has something that you want, for example, or that the only reason not to steal would be the likelihood of being caught. If young people often get into trouble it will be necessary to explore separately whether they understand the difference between right and wrong and whether they are able to inhibit antisocial actions (the domain of Social Competence is intertwined with this domain).

In adolescence young people may also develop a more global empathy, for example, a concern for others in a more abstract way that is not just associated with people they are close to. They may, for example, show concern about environmental issues, world poverty, natural disasters and so on. This is an interest that maybe could be capitalised upon in developing interventions with adolescents.

Adolescents should have a 'theory of mind', that is they should know that other people have feelings and that other people's feelings about certain things may not be the same as their own. They should also have a language for feelings, both their own and others. They can describe situations that will elicit emotions that require more understanding of contextual factors, such as those that elicit pride, jealousy, worry, guilt and gratitude; they can also describe situations that elicit the complex emotions of disgust, relief, shame, surprise, curiosity, excitement and disappointment (Harris *et al.* 1987; Terwogt and Stegge 1998). They can also think *about* emotions, therefore have more understanding about the possibility of actively trying to change how one feels. The development of such empathy is a crucial building block for prosocial behaviour. Again, young people who exhibit empathy are less likely to demonstrate aggressive behaviour towards others (Goldstein 1999). They should have a well-developed conscience that does not rely on adult supervision and monitoring. So, they should demonstrate that they are:

(a) Thinking or reasoning (problem-solving, decision-making) in a rational way

(b) Showing an awareness of, and consideration for, the needs, interests, and feelings of others as well as oneself

(c)   Behaving constructively (i.e., in ways that benefit both self and others). (Goldstein 1999, p.305)

If these elements are not evident then it may be necessary to draw from the *Early Years* and *School Years* workbooks for suggestions for intervention.

There are several aspects of care-giving that are known to encourage the development of prosocial behaviour. Warm and secure attachment to a caregiver provides the basis for the development of empathy and for the understanding that others have feelings that can be influenced. If the attachment figure models kind behaviour then this is highly influential because young people imitate people they identify with. Young people also respond to clear rules and expectations of behaviour towards others; however in adolescence it is also important that young people are given explanations and reasons for limits and sanctions. Parents with young people who show prosocial behaviour tend to (Schaffer 1996; Zahn-Waxler, Radke-Yarrow and King 1979):

- provide clear rules and principles for behaviour, reward kindness, show disapproval of unkindness and explain the effects of hurting others

- present moral messages in an emotional, rather than calm manner

- attribute prosocial qualities to the young person by telling him or her frequently that they are kind and helpful

- model prosocial behaviour themselves

- provide empathic care-giving to the young person.

The indicator for mapping this area is the young person's behaviour towards others. This can be assessed by direct observation, discussions with parents, teachers, keyworkers and carers, and conversations with the young person. Moral reasoning can be assessed by using simple vignettes posing moral dilemmas. It should be possible to check young people's ability to take the perspective of others by discussing with them how they think others might feel in different situations, for example, when the victim of a crime.

If a young person is already demonstrating positive actions towards others then this is very hopeful. It indicates a level of empathy, which in turn can be linked with self-esteem and an understanding that other people have feelings. The Search Institute, in Minneapolis, has carried out extensive work on what it describes as 'assets' factors that are similar and overlap with resilience factors. It has demonstrated that the more assets that teenagers have, including positive values, the less likely they are to become involved in high-risk behaviours (Search Institute 1997). Therefore, prosocial behaviour should be reinforced wherever possible and intervention to boost resilience can be built upon existing positive values, for example, by involving the young person in helping in a community project.

If a young person is not demonstrating positive values, then this should be considered a priority area for targeted intervention to boost resilience. The ecological model is highly important here because the social environment exerts such a strong influence over young people's social behaviour. The peer group, for example, is important for adolescents and the types of friendships made have a strong influence upon behaviour (see Friendships domain). Situations need to be created that require young people to care for and be responsible towards others. Empathic behaviour can be enhanced through encouraging interest in some of the environmental or charitable projects that interest teenagers.

Foster parents, teachers and other professionals in a caring role need to be able to put over the emotional messages when giving challenging messages about antisocial, unkind or cruel behaviour towards others. Although the professional role often requires calmness, and acceptance, this has to be balanced with the 'human' elements of an adult–young person relationship that foster empathy and positive values.

The starting point should be an assumption that everyone has the potential to behave prosocially and that no matter what traumas have been experienced, all young people can learn to control antisocial behaviour.

POSITIVE VALUES CHECKLIST
YOUNG PERSON

What level of moral reasoning does this young person show, what understanding of his or her own feelings and what ability to empathise with others?

1. A moral dilemma is provided below, including examples of possible replies at different levels of moral reasoning. Other dilemmas could be created as appropriate for the specific young person. Discuss the dilemma with the young person. Remember, it is the *reasons* that young people give for their responses that tell you most about their moral reasoning, not the actual answer.

2. Choose situations from this young person's own experience in which he or she has been in trouble for behaving antisocially, for example, where the young person has been picked up by the police for delinquent or antisocial behaviour. Have a discussion that focuses specifically on exploring his or her level of moral reasoning, for example, when a young person has been caught shoplifting some questions could be:

    (a) Why do you think the police were called?

         (example of 'preconventional' response: 'because I was recognised'; example of 'conventional' response: 'because I broke the law')

    (b) If you were the shopkeeper, what would you have done?

         (example of 'preconventional' response: 'made me give the things back'; example of 'conventional' response: 'called the police because I broke the law')

✓

(c) Why do you think people get punished for stealing?

(example of 'preconventional' response: 'because they get caught'; example of 'conventional' response: 'because if there were no rules against stealing the shops couldn't keep going')

(d) Do you think it is important to tell the truth, when you have been caught?

(example of 'preconventional' response: 'only if you can't get away with lying'; example of 'conventional' response: 'yes, because people don't like a liar').

3. Use the pictures 'Emotional faces' that follow with adolescents who appear to have a very limited understanding of emotions and how people express them. Assess whether they have the language to talk about emotions.

4. Again, for young people who have difficulty with emotions and understanding them use the pictures 'Emotional scenes' that follow as a basis for discussion.

5. Use the 'Index of empathy' checklist that follows to assess the extent to which the young person is able to take the perspective of others.

Ask the young person:

1. Do you ever find it difficult to let others know how you are feeling?

2. Do you ever have difficulty in knowing what other people are feeling?

3. What sort of thing would make someone:

(a) shy

(b) proud

(c) jealous

(d) worried

(e) guilty

(f) grateful

(g) disgusted

(h) relieved

(i) ashamed

(j)   surprised

(k)   curious

(l)   excited

(m)   disappointed?

What level of helping behaviour does this young person show?

Ask the young person:

1.   Are there any chores that you have to do:

(a)   at home

(b)   in placement

(c)   at school?

2.   Do you think there are other chores that you could do?

3.   Do you ever offer to help your parent or carer without being asked?

What level of comforting or sharing or more general prosocial behaviour does this young person show?

Arrange to observe directly the young person in school or college or with a group of peers and look for examples of prosocial behaviour. For example, how does the young person react when another person is upset or angry; does he or she share with others; does the young person help others who are struggling with an activity or task?

Ask the young person:

1.   Think about all the things that you are interested in and like; are there ways you could help another young person who is interested in the same things?

2.   Can you think of some ways in which you do help:

(a)   people that you know

(b)   local organisations (e.g. children's hospital, pet rescue etc.)

(c)   other people in the world (e.g. charities, Red Nose Day etc.)?

3.   Are there any of these that you would like to do, if you don't already?

4.   Do you already do, or would you like to try any of these:

(a)   gardening

(b)   planting trees

(c)   helping younger children

(d)   caring for animals

(e)   gathering litter?

MORAL DILEMMA

You have a Saturday job in a supermarket and you notice one of your classmates in the store. They put some things in a basket, but you see them shoplift something else. What would you do and why?

Options can include:

- tell them you saw them and ask them to pay
- tell the store manager
- not tell
- ask them to get things for you as well
- not tell, but ask your parents that night for advice.

Explore the reasoning by posing a number of questions and dilemmas such as:

1. What if the shoplifter is your best friend?

2. What if you know that the shoplifter is from a very poor family and you think he or she is getting a present for a family member?

3. What if he or she begs you not to tell and that they won't do it again?

4. What if he or she says they'll tell all your friends that you are a sneak and telltale or a spoilsport?

5. What if he or she says that the company is rich and they rip people off anyway?

6. What if the store manager is mean and has just refused all the Saturday helpers a pay rise?

✓

EMOTIONAL FACES

Emotional faces legends

Happy

Sad

Frightened

Angry

Adolescence, © Brigid Daniel and Sally Wassell 2002 © Iain Campbell 2002

Emotional faces legends

Bored

Guilty

Anxious

Proud

Ashamed

Shocked

Surprised

Puzzled

Adolescence, © Brigid Daniel and Sally Wassell 2002 © Iain Campbell 2002

✓

EMOTIONAL SCENES

Adolescence, © Brigid Daniel and Sally Wassell 2002 © Iain Campbell 2002

Emotional scenes legends

Frightened

Happy

Angry

Sad

AN INDEX OF EMPATHY FOR CHILDREN AND ADOLESCENTS

Adapted, with permission, from B. K. Bryant (1982) 'An index of empathy for children and adolescents.' *Child Development 53*, 413–425.

Administration

It is recommended that you go through the statements one-by-one with the young person to make sure he or she understands them. Each reply should be marked as a YES or NO in the answer column. Take care with the statements that are framed negatively to be sure they are understood. Some statements are framed in the negative so that each one has to be thought about, and the young person does not just answer YES to all. Do not try to add up the scores as you go along; do this afterwards.

Scoring

Using the scoring sheet, score 1 point for each YES reply to positive (+) item and score 1 point for each NO reply to a negative (-) item. For the rest score 0. Then add all the scores up to give a final total out of 22.

As a guide, when this test was validated with children in the US (Bryant 1982) the average (rounded) scores were as follows:

Boys: Grade 1–12, Grade 4–11, Grade 7–13

Girls: Grade 1–14, Grade 4–14, Grade 7–16

✓

Checklist

STATEMENT	RESPONSE YES or NO
1. It makes me sad to see a girl who can't find anyone to play with.	
2. People who kiss and hug in public are silly.	
3. Boys who cry because they are happy are silly.	
4. I really like to watch people open presents, even when I don't get a present myself.	
5. Seeing a boy who is crying makes me feel like crying.	
6. I get upset when I see a girl being hurt.	
7. Even when I don't know why someone is laughing, I laugh too.	
8. Sometimes I cry when I watch TV.	
9. Girls who cry because they are happy are silly.	
10. It's hard for me to see why someone else gets upset.	
11. I get upset when I see an animal being hurt.	
12. It makes me sad to see a boy who can't find anyone to play with.	
13. Some songs make me feel so sad I feel like crying.	
14. I get upset when I see a boy being hurt.	
15. Grown-ups sometimes cry even when they have nothing to be sad about.	
16. It's silly to treat dogs and cats as though they have feelings like people.	
17. I get angry when I see a classmate pretending to need help from the teacher all the time.	
18. Children who have no friends probably don't want any.	
19. Seeing a girl who is crying makes me feel like crying.	
20. I think it is funny that some people cry during a sad film or while reading a sad book.	
21. I am able to eat all my sweets even when I see someone looking at me wanting one.	
22. I don't feel upset when I see a classmate being punished by a teacher for not obeying school rule.	

Scoring sheet

	STATEMENT	SCORE GUIDE	SCORE
1.	It makes me sad to see a girl who can't find anyone to play with.	+ Score 1 for YES	
2.	People who kiss and hug in public are silly.	- Score 1 for NO	
3.	Boys who cry because they are happy are silly.	- Score 1 for NO	
4.	I really like to watch people open presents, even when I don't get a present myself.	+ Score 1 for YES	
5.	Seeing a boy who is crying makes me feel like crying.	+ Score 1 for YES	
6.	I get upset when I see a girl being hurt.	+ Score 1 for YES	
7.	Even when I don't know why someone is laughing, I laugh too.	+ Score 1 for YES	
8.	Sometimes I cry when I watch TV.	+ Score 1 for YES	
9.	Girls who cry because they are happy are silly.	- Score 1 for NO	
10.	It's hard for me to see why someone else gets upset.	- Score 1 for NO	
11.	I get upset when I see an animal being hurt.	+ Score 1 for YES	
12.	It makes me sad to see a boy who can't find anyone to play with.	+ Score 1 for YES	
13.	Some songs make me feel so sad I feel like crying.	+ Score 1 for YES	
14.	I get upset when I see a boy being hurt.	+ Score 1 for YES	
15.	Grown-ups sometimes cry even when they have nothing to be sad about.	- Score 1 for NO	
16.	It's silly to treat dogs and cats as though they have feelings like people.	- Score 1 for NO	
17.	I get angry when I see a classmate pretending to need help from the teacher all the time.	- Score 1 for NO	

18. Children who have no friends probably don't want any.	- Score 1 for NO	
19. Seeing a girl who is crying makes me feel like crying.	+ Score 1 for YES	
20. I think it is funny that some people cry during a sad film or while reading a sad book.	- Score 1 for NO	
21. I am able to eat all my sweets even when I see someone looking at me wanting one.	- Score 1 for NO	
22. I don't feel upset when I see a classmate being punished by a teacher for not obeying school rule.	- Score 1 for NO	
TOTAL SCORE		

POSITIVE VALUES CHECKLIST
PARENT/CARER

What level of moral reasoning does this young person show and what understanding of his or her own feelings and empathy with those of people close to the young person?

Ask anyone who knows the young person well about his or her understanding of morality. If necessary, describe the different stages of moral reasoning to them.

Ask the parent/carer:

1. To what extent do you think this young person is able to understand why there are rules and sanctions or does he or she judge actions entirely by outcome?

2. Does this young person show a respect for rules?

3. Does this young person appear to understand the importance of the intention behind behaviour, in other words, can he or she distinguish between accidental and deliberate harm?

4. To what extent can this young person take the perspective of others?

5. What emotions does this young person appear to recognise in others?

6. What emotion words does this young person have and are they used appropriately about him or herself?

7. Is this young person able to let you know how he or she is feeling?

8. Does this young person ever have difficulty knowing what others are feeling?

How does the parent or care environment encourage helping behaviour?

Ask the parent/carer:

1. Are there any chores that the young person is expected to carry out:

   (a) at home

   (b) in placement

   (c) at school?

2. How does the young person usually respond when asked to help?

3. Does the young person ever spontaneously offer to help?

4. What do you do if the young person does not help when asked?

What level of comforting or sharing or more general prosocial behaviour does this young person show?

Ask the parent/carer:

1. When this young person is with other children and young people, how does he or she react if another person is distressed, either because of their own or another young person's actions or an accident? Have you seen this young person try to comfort others?

2. Have you seen the young person spontaneously share his or her possessions or activities with others?

3. How does he or she usually react if another young person asks to borrow something of theirs, for example a CD or computer game?

4. What opportunity can be created for this young person to take responsibility for someone else's welfare, for example:

   (a) mentor for newcomer at school

   (b) helper for new young person in residential unit

   (c) guide for young person new to activity in which this young person is already skilled?

8

Social Competencies

Background information

The capacity for social competence has been demonstrated to be associated with resilience (Luthar 1991; Werner and Smith 1992). It is very difficult to pin down 'social competence' because it covers such a wide range of skills and attributes, many of them very closely intertwined with those associated with the Positive Values and Friendships domains. A useful definition is that developed by a Scottish Executive funded initiative, the Promoting Social Competence project based at Dundee University (Promoting Social Competence 1999):

> Social Competence is possessing and using the ability to integrate thinking, feeling and behaviour to achieve social tasks and outcomes valued in the host context and culture.

The definition goes on to incorporate:

> perception of relevant social cues, interpretation of social cues, realistic anticipation of obstacles to personally desired behaviour, anticipation of consequences of behaviour for self and others, generation of effective solutions to interpersonal problems, translation of social decisions into effective social behaviours, and the expression of a positive sense of self-efficacy.

Bernard (1991) identifies a group of factors that indicate resilience:

- social competence

- autonomy, also known as internal locus of control

- capacity for problem-solving

- sense of purpose and future.

The foundations for social competence are laid in early childhood. During early years children begin to develop autonomy and self-control. Autonomy describes the ability to operate as an independent individual and underpins social competence. It is during adolescence that a re-emergence of a struggle for autonomy can often be observed (Steinberg 1993). With the development of appropriate autonomy young people increasingly learn how to master the social and physical world and develop a sense of self-efficacy. They learn about social and moral rules and compliance with parental expectations. They become better at directing their attention, focusing their attention and persisting in attendance on tasks (Masten, Best and Garmezy 1990).

By adolescence young people's sense of self-efficacy will be shaped and will affect their interactions with their peers and with adults. The development of self-efficacy depends in part upon the development of accurate explanations for events and the behaviour of oneself and others. These 'attributions', as they are known, have three components (Petersen and Seligman 1985). The first is whether the cause for an event is attributed to internal characteristics of the person, or to external, situational factors. For example, a young person apparently ignores another young person who could make the internal attribution 'They've deliberately ignored me', or the external attribution 'They've not seen me'. The second component is whether the cause is seen as stable over time or transient: 'They're always going to ignore me' or 'This is just a one-off'. The third component concerns whether the cause is seen to apply globally or specifically: 'Other people are going to start ignoring me' or 'It is only this person who's ignored me'. As they mature young people need to develop reasonably accurate attributions about their own and others' behaviour. Young people who have suffered abuse or severe loss often develop attributions that are internal, stable and global: 'It's my fault, it's going to last forever and it will affect everything I do'.

During adolescence cognitive skills should be maturing so that young people become increasingly sophisticated in their ability to take another's perspective and to consider the situational factors that affect events. They should be developing a range of problem-solving skills. Adolescents should have sufficient self-control to help them inhibit impulsive reactions to events. They should be developing a repertoire of social skills and should be aware of the social conventions, even if they challenge them at times.

During adolescence socially appropriate conduct is expected:

> One of the most important criteria by which children are evaluated by adults in their society is by their conduct with respect to rules or social norms for behaviour, the expectations teachers have for conduct in the classroom and on the playground, and the laws of society governing conduct. Children are described as well-behaved rather than disobedient, antisocial, or delinquent according to their compliance with these norms for social behaviour. (Masten *et al.* 1990, p.210)

Lack of social competence can be shown in different ways. Some adolescents are very withdrawn and lack the confidence and ability to engage with other young people and find it very difficult to communicate effectively with adults. Such young people are likely to have a low sense of self-efficacy and to lack communication and social skills. They may not attract the same level of attention as other young people, but their need for intervention is great. If, by adolescence, a young person is isolated and socially inept, he or she is likely to be increasingly ostracised or ignored with the result of further withdrawal from the activities of their peers.

Other young people show high levels of aggression which mean that they fall out with their peers and may move into delinquent acts and law-breaking. Long-term studies have shown that aggression in childhood can persist and become associated with criminal activities, violence to others and antisocial behaviour in late adolescence and into adulthood (Farrington 1991). During school years the levels of instrumental aggression (that is aggression aimed at getting what you want) normally declines. As older children develop the ability to put themselves in another's place and to understand the reasons behind other people's actions there should be a reduction of aggression. However, for adolescents lacking in social competencies aggression can become more subtle and deliberately planned (Schaffer 1996).

If a young person is showing rule-breaking behaviour in school years it is very likely to persist into adolescence, unless there is prompt and appropriate intervention (Masten *et al.* 1990). There is a strong association between academic achievement and rule-governed behaviour, but the direction of causality is not clear. Low IQ and lack of achievement could lead to frustration and alienation and therefore aggressive and antisocial behaviour. Alternatively, aggressive and antisocial behaviour could interfere with learning processes. It seems that in adolescence the direction is that antisocial problems may be more likely to interfere with learning therefore intervention aimed at behaviour control is an essential part of prevention of further social competence difficulties (Masten *et al.* 1990).

Adolescents should have a sense of purpose and future as well as the knowledge that they can have an influence upon the future shape of their lives. It is the life choices that young people make, such as whether to continue with education, whether to marry young, what peer group to mix with, whether to have children and so on, that are highly influenced by previous experience, and also influence long-term outcomes. What distinguishes resilient young people is their knowledge that they can make choices that counteract the adversity they have suffered. Social competence facilitates sensible decision-making.

Social skills involve cognitive, affective and behavioural aspects, therefore, when assessing them there needs to be attention to the *cognitive* areas like:

- planning and decision-making
- understanding cause and effect
- reflection
- problem-solving

affective areas like:

- empathy
- ability to take the perspective of others
- pleasure in having friends

behavioural areas like:

- interpersonal competence
- able to inhibit instinctive response
- conflict resolution.

SOCIAL COMPETENCIES CHECKLIST
YOUNG PERSON

As described in the introduction, the term 'social competence' covers a wide range of cognitive, affective and behavioural factors. The focus here will primarily be upon cognitive and behavioural aspects of social competence because the affective aspects are essentially assessed in the Positive Values domain. Peer relationships are obviously a crucial indicator of social competence and although touched on here are assessed in detail in the Friendships domain.

To what extent do this young person's personal characteristics contribute to his or her level of social competence?

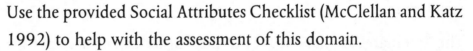

Use the provided Social Attributes Checklist (McClellan and Katz 1992) to help with the assessment of this domain.

Ask the young person about the following aspects of social competence.

AUTONOMY

Are you able to make the kinds of decisions about your life that you want to (for example, choosing friends, deciding how to spend free time, earning and spending your own money)?

SELF-CONTROL/PROBLEM-SOLVING

1. Do you ever worry that you can't control your temper?

2. Do you ever find yourself hitting out at other people without really thinking about it?

3. Do you ever feel that you don't show your feelings enough?

4. Do you ever feel that you show your feelings too much?

5. When you are in a difficult situation, can you usually think of different ways you could react and decide which seems the best (for example, if you ask to stay out overnight and your parent or carer objects, your choices could include just staying out anyway; suggesting that you arrange for the parents of your friend you want to stay with to phone your parent or carer; agree not to stay out)?

TEMPERAMENT

1. Do you think of yourself as a cheerful sort of person?

2. What kind of sense of humour do you have (for example, do you make jokes, do you usually get other people's jokes)?

3. If something goes wrong for you, for example if you ask someone out and they turn you down, do you usually get over it quite quickly, or does it take you a long time to stop feeling upset?

4. If an adult you don't know very well, perhaps a teacher of another class or a distant relative, speaks to you, how do you usually feel (for example, shy, pleased, nervous, chatty)?

SELF-EFFICACY

The 'Internal/External Locus of Control Scale' can be used as a gauge for the level of self-efficacy that the young person shows. Either use it in full as it stands, or use it as a basis for areas to discuss.

ATTENTION

1. Do you find that you get distracted easily from things like working at school, or watching the TV?

2. Are you usually able to concentrate on a difficult task until it is finished?

SENSE OF PURPOSE AND FUTURE

1. Do you look forward to the next few years?

2. Can you imagine what you might be doing?

3. Do you feel generally hopeful about how your life is going?

To what extent does the parent or carer environment encourage social competencies?

Ask the young person:

1. What sort of rules are there in your house about getting on with each other (for example, saying 'please' and 'thank you', answering when spoken to or asked a question, being told not to interrupt others, helping out)?

2. How do your parents or carers usually react if you do something wrong? Do they explain to you why it is wrong, what sort of punishments do you get, do you usually know what things will annoy them?

What opportunities does this young person have to develop competence in a wider social environment?

Ask the young person:

1. Do you spend as much time as you would like with other young people your age?

2. Do you usually get on OK with other young people?

3. Do you find that you fall out with friends easily?

4. What do your parents or carers do or say if you fall out with your friends?

5. Can you usually get through the school/college/work day without being told off for something?

6. Do you find the school/college/work rules easy to keep (for example, if there is a uniform, not eating in class, not shouting out, lining up when told, and son on)?

✓

SOCIAL ATTRIBUTES CHECKLIST

This checklist (McClellan and Katz 1992) is available on the internet from the ERIC Digest at http://www.ed.gov/databases/ERIC_Digests/index/. Items on the digest are for public use and there is a range of articles relating to resilience that may be of use.

Individual attributes

The child:

1. Is USUALLY in a positive mood

2. Is not EXCESSIVELY dependent on the teacher, assistant or other adults

3. USUALLY comes to the program or setting willingly

4. USUALLY copes with rebuffs and reverses adequately

5. Shows the capacity to empathise

6. Has positive relationship with one or two peers; shows capacity to really care about them, miss them if absent, etc.

7. Displays the capacity for humour

8. Does not seem to be acutely or chronically lonely.

Social skills attributes

The child USUALLY:

1. Approaches others positively

2. Expresses wishes and preferences clearly; gives reasons for actions and positions

3. Asserts own rights and needs appropriately

4. Is not easily intimidated by bullies

5. Expresses frustrations and anger effectively and without harming others or property

6. Gains access to ongoing groups at play and work

7. Enters ongoing discussion on the subject; makes relevant contributions to ongoing activities

8. Takes turns fairly easily

Adolescence, © Brigid Daniel and Sally Wassell 2002 © Iain Campbell 2002

9. Shows interest in others; exchanges information with and requests information from others appropriately

10. Negotiates and compromises with others appropriately

11. Does not draw inappropriate attention to self

12. Accepts and enjoys peers and adults of ethnic groups other than his or her own

13. Interacts non-verbally with other children with smiles, waves, nods, etc.

Peer relationship attributes

The child is:

1. USUALLY accepted versus neglected or rejected by other children

2. SOMETIMES invited by other children to join them in play, friendship and work.

✓

INTERNAL/EXTERNAL LOCUS OF CONTROL SCALE

The Nowicki-Strickland Internal/External Locus of Control Scale has been adapted into a shorter form for young people. Reproduced with the permission of Steve Nowicki.

I'd like to ask you some questions now. There are no right or wrong answers. I'm just interested in knowing what you think and feel about different things.

	YES/NO
Do you feel that wishing can make good things happen?	
Are people nice to you no matter what you do?	
Do you usually do badly in your school work even when you try hard?	
When a friend is angry with you is it hard to make that friend like you again?	
Are you surprised when your teacher praises you for your work? (Prompt: if children say teacher hasn't praised them yet, ask about previous teacher – and note down in comments below)	
When bad things happen to you is it usually someone else's fault?	
Is doing well in your class work just a matter of 'luck' for you?	
Are you often blamed for things that just aren't your fault?	
When you get into an argument or fight is it usually the other person's fault?	
Do you think that preparing for tests is a waste of time?	
When nice things happen to you is it usually because of 'luck'?	
Does planning ahead make good things happen?	
Comments	

Adolescence, © Brigid Daniel and Sally Wassell 2002 © Iain Campbell 2002

Internal/External Locus Of Control Scale Scoring

First reverse the score of the last question, i.e. if the young person says 'yes' to the last question, change it to 'no'. Then count up the number of 'yes' replies and the number of 'no' replies.

EXTERNAL Locus of Control (i.e. young person tends to see events as being controlled by external forces, has a low sense of self-efficacy) is associated with having more 'YES' scores.

INTERNAL Locus of Control (i.e. young person tends to see him or herself as having some control over events, has a high sense of self-efficacy) is associated with having more 'NO' scores.

✓

SOCIAL COMPETENCIES CHECKLIST
PARENT/CARER

To what extent do this young person's personal characteristics contribute to his or her level of social competence?

The Social Attributes Checklist (McClellan and Katz 1992) can be used with the parent or carer to find out their view of their child's social competence.

Ask the parent/carer about the following aspects of social competence.

AUTONOMY

What opportunities are there for the young person to try things for him or herself and to make some of their own decisions (for example, choosing friends, deciding how to spend free time, earning and spending their own money)?

SELF-CONTROL/PROBLEM-SOLVING

Does the young person exert some measure of control over his or her behaviour, at a level that can normally be expected of an adolescent, does he or she show excessive levels of aggression? Does he or she appear to have any level of control over different possible reactions to a given situation?

TEMPERAMENT

Is the young person normally cheerful, does she or he demonstrate a sense of humour, can he or she be comforted after a set-back, does he or she respond openly to overtures from adults and so on?

SELF-EFFICACY

The parent or carer can be asked how they would consider the child would rate on each item of the 'Internal/External Locus of Control Scale'.

Adolescence, © Brigid Daniel and Sally Wassell 2002 © Iain Campbell 2002

ATTENTION

Can the young person concentrate for periods of time on a particular task, can the young person be encouraged to read a book, will he or she watch a video right through, will he or she make a number of attempts to complete a difficult task?

SENSE OF PURPOSE AND FUTURE

Does the young person appear to look forward to the next few years? Does he or she ever talk about what he or she might be doing? Does he or she seem to be generally hopeful about how his or her life is going?

To what extent does the parent or carer environment encourage social competencies?

Ask the parent/carer:

1. What aspects of social behaviour do you believe to be important and how do you encourage such behaviour (for example saying 'please' and 'thank you', responding when greeted or asked a question, learning not to interrupt others, looking at people when they address him or her, turn-taking in conversation and games, responding when asked to help out)?

2. What is your approach to discipline (for example, do you explain the reasons for your decisions, can you separate disapproval of the behaviour from feelings about the child)?

What opportunities does this young person have to develop competence in a wider social environment?

Ask the parent/carer:

1. Does this young person have the opportunity to spend time with other young people of about his or her own age?

2. How would you deal with a situation where the young person has fallen out with a friend?

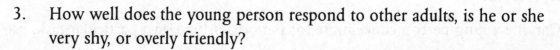

3. How well does the young person respond to other adults, is he or she very shy, or overly friendly?

4. Does he or she appear to understand the school/college/work rules and conventions?

5. Does he or she manage to keep to the school/college/work rules and conventions in a reasonable way?

Part II

Intervention

9

Intervention Strategies

Introduction

It is beyond the scope of these workbooks to give comprehensive intervention guidance. By its very nature, practice that aims to promote resilience has to be individually tailored to suit each individual young person and his or her unique circumstances. Instead, principles to underpin the planning of intervention are outlined and for each domain examples of possible intervention strategies are provided. Practitioners are encouraged to be as creative as possible in developing these strategies further to meet individual needs.

The balancing act

It can be difficult to decide whether to build upon existing strengths or whether to concentrate on boosting areas of less strength. Five strategies for intervention have been suggested (Masten 1994):

- reduce vulnerability and risk

- reduce the number of stressors and pile-up

- increase the available resources

- mobilise protective processes

- foster resilience strings (where an improvement in one domain has a positive knock-on effect in other domains).

We would recommend that practitioners strive to strike a balance between these different approaches. Current practice is frequently characterised by risk reduction and therefore more attention may need to be paid to looking for strengths and building upon them. Wherever possible a strength in one domain can be used to boost a weaker domain. For example, if a young person has a strong attachment to a member of the extended family (Secure Base = strong), but takes part in no activities or hobbies (Talents and Interests = weak), the attachment figure can be encouraged and supported in helping the young person to take part in an activity. Similarly, if a young person has a good friend (Friendships = strong), but misses a lot of school (Education = weak), consideration could be given to involving the friend in encouragement to attend, perhaps by arranging for them to travel together.

The holistic approach

The resilient young person can be described as one who can say (Grotberg 1997):

> I HAVE
>
> I AM
>
> I CAN

For example, the young person can say 'I have people who love me and people to help me', 'I am a likeable person and respectful of myself and others' and 'I can find ways to solve problems and can control myself'. The three categories loosely equate with the three building blocks of secure base, self-esteem and self-efficacy. The aim of intervention would be to develop all the domains so that the young person can make such positive statements about him or herself:

> I HAVE: this could be boosted via work on Secure Base and Friendships
>
> I AM: this could be boosted via Positive Values and Social Competencies
>
> I CAN: this could be boosted via Education and Talents and Interests.

The ecological approach

As has been stressed throughout the workbook, consider interventions at each ecological level. The following practice suggestions are grouped, as far as possible, into each ecological level, although there may well be considerable overlap.

Multi-agency, network approach

Finally, it is essential that the social worker does not attempt to carry out work on all the domains alone.

Any professional involved with the young person and family must be involved in any planning discussions about boosting resilience and there must agreement about priorities and how to address them. For example, a residential keyworker may take the main role in working on talents and interests, but the school should also be informed of what these talents and interests are so that they can reinforce them.

The whole of the young person's network of family and friends should be assessed for potential to help with boosting resilience. For example, a grandparent may be able to offer time to help with homework, or a friend's parent may be able to include the young person on outings if given some financial help.

PRACTICE SUGGESTIONS
SECURE BASE

This domain of resilience acts as a focus for deliberate strategies fundamental to basic care routines for the young person. These often simple strategies, applied with persistence and consistency, can strengthen the young person's feeling of basic security and belonging. They may be introduced as a way of improving existing attachment relationships, or to help with the development of new ones. Although it is important for the young person to be attached to the main carer, this should not preclude attention to relationships with other important people in the young person's life. The improvement of attachment relationships will be most likely to promote healthy developmental progress and recovery from the impact of adversities. We need to examine:

- the existing sense of a secure base within the young person, and

- existing strengths in the family setting which can be harnessed, but also

- existing strengths in the community and professional resources.

A useful paradigm, as described above, defines the resilient young person as one who can make positive statements on each of three areas (Grotberg 1997):

I HAVE

I AM

I CAN

These three perspectives link particularly directly with interventions around the provision of a secure base, that is, when building security and predictability for young people. Promoting a sense in young people that they have relationships with significant people available to them and have a supportive environment is clearly relevant in the deliberate structuring of elements of the young person's environment focused on increasing a sense of security. Such interventions mirror the functions of a secure or 'good enough' attachment relationship that acts to reduce anxiety and to promote healthy exploration and learning in the young person at every stage of their development. They are highly relevant for work with adolescents who may have lost their secure base or who never experienced predictability and security of care at home.

Every element of the young person's environment may act to reassure the young person that he or she has available to them a net of security such as to communicate messages:

'I have reliable predictable adults available to me to offer support.'

'I have a reliable routine.'

The second helpful concept is the focus on the promotion of a sense of healthy identity as expressed in the phrase 'I am'. Attachment to a person who values the young person for his or her intrinsic qualities will facilitate the development of good self-esteem, that is the ability to say 'I am a person worthy of love and attention'.

Care-givers need to make detailed attempts to structure the young person's immediate care environment so as to make it possible for him or her to *achieve* in even a small way some aim which has salience for them. This may have particular importance, for example, for a young person who has no sense of initiative and such a poorly developed sense of self-concept that he or she does not even know what they enjoy and are capable of. We know that a sense of achievement is an important component of self-esteem, and that this is facilitated by the messages of acceptance communicated by all the elements of a secure base.

Finally, it is possible to progress from the notion of 'I have' in relation to basic security, to 'I can' in relation to achievement. In other words, the young person who has a basic sense of security is more likely to feel that he or she can attempt new tasks and explore the environment in the search for mastery, and later incorporate these positive experiences into a confident self-identity. This requires the integration of experiences, opportunities, successes and problem-solving skills to the point where the young person perceives these capacities and abilities as part of him or herself, not merely as a function of chance or a particular setting. It also provides a chance to establish and reinforce for each young person a sense of *mastery* and *autonomy*. This relates very closely to the notion of self-efficacy in that the young person who is confident in his or her ability is more likely to feel 'I can do something about the problems and difficulties I face'.

Whether the young person is at home or looked after by the local authority, a useful framework for planning intervention may be represented by the following questions:

1. What has happened to this young person?

2. What have been the messages to the young person in life events, relationships and circumstances?

3. What behaviour do we see, especially in persistent patterns?

4. What is this behaviour communicating?

5. What do we want to communicate?

6. How might we do this:

    (a) in the care routines for the young person

    (b) in any direct work which is done with the young person?

This provides a simple framework for reflection on the source of the behaviour problems. It is often helpful to separate intervention into addressing:

- the care routines or environment which need to be created for the young person

- the ways that positive behaviour can be promoted to build resilience

- the explanations that need to given to the young person and the best way to give them.

At the adolescent stage it is easy to assume that attachment relationships are less important in providing a sense of security as it is a time when the young person is striving for independence. However, we know that adolescence mirrors toddlerhood as the drive for assertion is often strong and is most securely pursued from the base of acceptance, belonging and support from important relationships with adults. Those young people with a poor basic sense of security may well be driven to avoid assertive action or to engage in risk taking to a dangerous level. Secure limits are needed, but in the context of a listening, respectful, inclusive attitude towards the young person.

> Family relationships remain essential to most young people. Even if they are not able to live at home many young people retain strong ties to family members, including extended family members. Careful assessment of the importance of the relationship is necessary without making assumptions about who is important. (Daniel *et al.* 1999, p.284)

Observing carefully and developing a picture of the young person's *wishes and feelings* is much more complicated than it may seem. For example, verbal statements and behaviour may conflict. The young person may want contact with someone who has harmed him or her or who may lead the young person into dangerous situations.

At this time issues of identity come to the fore. Opportunity for contact with people from the past are important at this stage and may be most helpfully promoted *before* the young person is living independently away from potential adult support. We know that many young people attempt to re-establish these contacts following lengthy periods of accommodation by the local authority. It is important to offer help to the young person with testing the value and reliability of these links, and the actual practical support they offer, in the context of continuing relationships, *before* he or she leaves the care setting.

Helping the young person to feel secure

1. Shape interventions deliberately in response to the young person's attachment style, and remember that persistence will be required. For example, a young person who avoids contact (avoidant attachment pattern) will need patiently available carers who do not press the young person to come close but whose availability to offer support is nevertheless predictably present. A young person who shows a combination of high levels of need for the carer combined with angry resistance (ambivalent attachment pattern) needs carers who have the patience and fortitude to withstand the demand and rejection: they need to help the young person through the urge to reject closeness. A young person whose responses are confused (disorganised attachment pattern) will need carers who can tolerate mixed responses and who are reliable and reassuring in their own responses. A young person who shows clinging, anxious preoccupation with presence of the attachment figure (anxious attachment pattern) needs reassurance of carer responses that are as *predictable* as it is possible to provide, with only gradual encouragement

in surviving brief separations. Downes (1992) has provided a helpful guide to foster carers looking after adolescents with different attachment patterns.

2. When promoting purposeful contact it can be helpful to *anticipate* potential problems and rehearse with the young person how they might deal with these. This provides the young person with problem-solving skills and also identifies that the helping adult is available to offer support, strategies and resources. It is important that the young person has knowledge that he or she has a secure base to return to and that emotional support above all else will be predictably available in at least one important relationship with another adult.

3. The parent or carer should take every opportunity, not only to *respond* to the young person's demonstrated distress and to support him or her when under stress but also to *reach out* to the young person to initiate positive experiences (Fahlberg 1991). It is not helpful simply to wait for the young person to voice concerns, as many young people will find this too difficult. It is vital that the carer or parent takes initiatives to protect the young person from undue negative effects of adverse circumstances.

4. When trying to understand any messages the young person may be giving about his or her assumptions as to why he or she is not at home, why someone important has left, or the reasons for any other negative life events, help the parent or carer to reflect upon the young person's *behaviour*, as well as what he or she *says*. Initiatives that encourage *reflection* with the young person about the reasons for decisions or life events can be powerfully protective against later difficulties.

5. Many young people may be able to explore through drama, music or role play events that have troubled them or about which they feel great confusion.

6. Any way in which the adult can communicate an *acceptance* to the young person of his or her individuality is likely to be of great value. During adolescence young people explore notions of self-identity and will incorporate the messages they receive from others into this identity. Therefore, those in contact with young people need to help them to feel that they are individuals of worth.

7. Provide the young person with time and space to talk about his or her experiences of loss and separation.

8.   Role play can be an effective way for young people to practise their skills in relating to other people, both peers and adults. Group role-play activities can be particularly effective.

Ensuring that the young person has a secure base

1.   Building healthier attachment relationships may be the most important initiative which, through work with parent and young person separately or the parent and young person relationship directly, can make a real difference to the young person's sense of security.

2.   An essential element of a secure base for young people is predictability of care. Steady routines can have a deeply reassuring affect and the reliable availability of those important to the young person provides a sense of belonging. Even though routines are thought to be particularly important for younger children, many adolescents who have had difficult early experiences are profoundly reassured by predictable routines in their care setting wherever this may be, either at home, in foster care or in residential care. A major skill of carers is to balance the predictability of routine and flexibility of responsiveness to the young person's individual needs or sense of initiative.

3.   Interest in the young person's activities, encouragement of the young person to take initiatives in play and development of the young person's autonomy, will build self-esteem.

4.   The young person who has difficulty separating needs to develop trust in the carer. Young people need explanations and reassurance about separation. The best way for them to develop trust in carers is through experience in them as reliable. So, if carers say that they will pick a young person up at a particular time, then they must stick to it.

5.   Taking opportunities for special rituals for each individual young person, at Christmas or other religious festivals, on their birthday and in celebration of significant achievements or events can build a trusting relationship between the young person and any significant adult.

6.   Any initiative and work with parents which helps them to learn about the developmental stage and actions they can take to increase the young person's sense of security will be invaluable. For example, reliable, predictable routines are often underestimated by parents who

themselves have had poor experiences of nurturing and group work support can help parents to understand about young people's needs. Adolescents are often considered to be able to look after themselves, but they still need to know that someone is caring for them.

7. It may also be possible to work with parents in group settings. One approach to group work focuses on helping parents to change the kind of attributions they make about their children's behaviour.

8. Any initiative, however small, that communicates to the young person that the adult has *space* and *time* for him or her and that they are unique and special in their own way, is likely to communicate a message of positive regard. Predictable periods of time spent with the young person by a caring adult offering praise and encouragement and affirmation can be of vital significance. For example, regular participation in a joint activity can help in this.

9. In residential or foster care settings, it is very important to offer the young person regular private time to reflect on issues of concern. It may be easier for this to happen spontaneously in a foster care setting. Depending on the culture within a unit, some young people may keep a low profile much of the time, especially if they have learned to hide their emotional needs. The provision of a regular predictable period of time each week with an important staff member or keyworker can be invaluable in modelling a secure base in which the young person can rely upon the relationship with the adults to raise issues of underlying concern.

10. Whatever the young person's living setting, he or she will need the comfort of contact with important people from his or her past and present: to have a notion that 'I have adults available to me when I need them'. Contact, if the young person is separated from attachment figures, needs to be *purposeful* so that it aims to meet the young person's needs. It is also important to consult with the family about *how* contact can be prepared for and effectively managed. On home visits young people often want to be out with peers, not with their parents. Therefore, time with peers needs to be built into the contact to accommodate this. Active gaining of *permission* from parents is vital here, even if it takes time, as it can consolidate the secure base both in the present placement and future care settings if the young person knows that the parent is able to communicate their approval.

11. Photographs, tapes, drawings and videos can all help to keep important memories of life for young people and remind them of their roots and sense of belonging in their community.

12. The way in which the local authority carries out its procedures in relationship to *all* the work undertaken with young people and families communicates powerful messages as to the way in which the contribution of family members is welcomed, valued and used. For example, there are many opportunities when a young person is preparing to move home, unless this is an emergency, for establishing good links with new carers and offering the parents an opportunity to explore their worries and concerns. Clarifying as early as possible the arrangements for contact, particularly at the first meeting, will have vital significance for the young person and give a strong message to the family as to their importance in his or her life. Empowering the family by sharing as much information as possible with them will do much to keep them involved. It is important to reflect upon:

    (a) How they might be involved in the young person's admission to local authority accommodation.

    (b) How they may be involved in reviews.

    (c) How they may be kept informed of important elements of the young person's life, for example, school progress, activities.

13. More work may need to be done with the adults, for example, when there are warring, separated parents, than directly with the young people in establishing the young person's right to contact with an important person who has left the household.

Capitalising upon the wider resources that are available as an attachment network

1. Base deliberate plans for care and contact upon careful attention to young people's wishes and feelings to counteract both feelings of powerlessness and those of self-blame. Take care in thinking through with the young person wherever possible  *who* is important so that opportunities to sustain and build important attachments can be maintained, despite separations. For young people who are accommodated on a long-term basis, past contacts may be all the more important. It is therefore helpful to sustain links with past

carers wherever this is at all possible and thereby promote a sense of continuity in the young person's experience.

2. It may be that important people to the young person are overlooked when making the care plan, or their significance minimised. It may be assumed that the young person's mother is more important when a grandparent or father may be of real significance. Make no assumptions about who has something to offer the young person. It could be very reassuring for an adolescent to develop or maintain a sense of being part of a bigger family network. Finding a resourceful adult who has survived adversity with skill and ingenuity can be deeply comforting to adolescents who are temporarily at sea in their own lives. There may be many benefits to convening a family group conference or a family network meeting. Through such an initiative, it may well be possible to find 'lost' adults who are able to offer contact, activities or other support, even though they are not able to accommodate the young person.

3. Peer relationships at this stage of development are of particular importance and *retaining* peer links can be helpful, not only in reassuring them if they have to move, but also in retaining links preparatory to a move home.

4. Assess the nature and strength of sibling bonds and reassess this in the light of reparative work and care. For example, for a sibling group where conflict has been a necessary adaptation to difficult family circumstances, or where there is an unhelpful allocation of roles to individual young people, special attention to building mutual empathy may be invaluable. For example, an older sibling who completely takes over a younger person as a result of poor overall nurturing of all the young people can be released from this responsibility. The aims here might be:

    (a) rewarding 'required helpfulness', while

    (b) encouraging the older sibling to relinquish elements of the caring role which detract from their own healthy development, and

    (c) encouraging age-appropriate initiatives for the older sibling and assertion in the younger person.

5. Ensure that the parents are provided with the financial and material resources that they need to support them in their parenting. This will include ensuring that all due benefits are applied for, that the housing

department keeps the house upgraded, that job opportunities are available and so on.

6. Resources available to support parents of young people within the community can be vital sources of help, especially for isolated, vulnerable parents. Consideration needs to be given to the parents' current personal resources when making plans for support initiatives. For example, where parents are depressed, making new social links may be very difficult for them, so keeping support initiatives focused and confined helps to minimise the emotional demands on them (Thompson 1995).

7. Foster carers are key adults with members of their local communities in encouraging young people to make the most of their abilities and capacities. They often have important links with community activities in which the young person can take part. For example, one foster family has a core role in the organisation of the local gala day to which they contribute much energy, creativity and commitment each year. The young people in the placement have the opportunity to be involved in all kinds of activities that contribute to this community day. Many young people in this placement have benefited from such opportunities as the activities organised range from sports to cooking and running a crèche.

8. It is important to keep a very strong link with the school, not only for the benefits that will come from the young person's education, but also for the sense of belonging and security that it can promote. This can be very powerful for young people living in adversity at home, for example, struggling with the impact of domestic violence.

9. Facilitating contact with any important person to the young person promotes a sense of continuity and therefore strengthens the sense of secure base.

10. For the young person who is at home, it may be that there is an important neighbour who can be encouraged to have consistent nurturing individual contact with the young person.

11. Try to organise for continuity of availability of any professionals involved with the child.

12. There may well be important people for the young person from their community of origin who can provide a great deal of support to them through adversity. These people may be voluntary youth workers,

neighbours, adults linked with local clubs who can retain a link with any young person who is temporarily or long-term accommodated away from home. These adults may link with them over a favourite activity, for example, football, gymnastics or singing or they may be more clearly focused on social skills development.

13. It may be very helpful to find a befriender or a mentor for the young person; even if he or she has important attachment relationships within their families, the mentor relationship can enhancing the young person's network rather than replacing links with family members.

14. For young people who come from minority ethnic or cultural groups, it is vitally important that the links with their culture remain wherever possible. These links need to be given positive value by those caring for young people from different communities if they have to be separated from their birth and extended families. Involvement of the young person in familiar religious or cultural events or routines can reassure the young person that his or her origins are valued by those caring for them. Such rituals as the preparation of familiar foods give powerful positive messages about the young person's culture.

15. Every opportunity needs to be taken with young people in communicating an acceptance of *difference*. This is especially important for young people who come from minority social groupings and therefore may already be experiencing prejudice and even rejection. Creative and energetic initiatives from carers in order to maintain cultural links can work against the feeling of stigmatisation in care settings and isolation from a black young person's community of origin. For example, a male professional in a large British city became aware that a number of young males from his own ethnic community were 'failing' at school. He joined forces with other adults who were similarly concerned about this and they ran and have since maintained a local support group for these young people, focusing on education, but building a broader sense of esteem in the young people they work with.

A number of suggestions of messages that can be given to young people in residential care settings and how they may be communicated are contained in Table 9.1.

Table 9.1 Giving messages to young people in residential care settings

Messages	How they are sent
We accept that you will make mistakes.	Verbal reassurance, opportunity to learn from mistakes, no automatic discharge, modelling.
You are not your behaviour.	Language used in reprimands.
We value you.	Showing encouragement, interest in them, listening. Nice physical environment, investment in space.
You should have expectations and hopes.	Using care plan, attainable, realistic goals, valuing agreement, resourcing talents and interests.
You have a voice which will be listened to.	Listening, children's meetings, confidentiality, involving in care plan, complaints and child friendly meetings.
You must have respect for and keep safe other young people and staff.	Challenging unacceptable behaviour, caring culture, modelling realistic consequences, re-educating in how to express in other ways.
You will always be warm, fed and kept healthy during your stay.	Proving physical environment, choice, personalised spaces, routine, access to preventative health care, information on keeping self healthy.
You should not be physically/socially/emotionally abused.	Open culture, trained/experienced staff, enough staff, voice in admissions/discharge, good supervision.
We like you.	Giving verbal and physical affection, choosing to spend time with them, praise, fun, surviving difficult times together.
We want you to understand what is happening.	Keyworker, information packs/tapes, involvement in meeting/reports.
We want you to feel safe.	Own room and keys, health and safety, open culture, proactive questions: 'do you feel safe?' call cards when from outside.
We want you to feel you have choices.	Involving in planning, giving *real* choices, honesty about their part in decision-making.

We want you to feel you have responsibilities.	Giving responsibilities, allowing them to take risks, increasing independence with age/ability, integrating 'through care' training into placement.
We want you to move on positively.	Good linking to next place and last place, good planning, celebrating main event, being welcomed back.
We want you to know that we will continue to care and be interested in you once you leave.	After care, staff outreach, welcome back young person, 'crashpad', inviting to key occasions, showing that staff continue to be interested in ex-residents, being on the end of the phone.
We want you to build positive relationships.	Resolving conflict rather than punishing. Teaching skills, modelling, supporting in outside relationships: 'It's OK not to like everyone'.
We will be interested in your *whole* life story.	Life-story work, being motivated to gather information, making good links with outside, listening to them, respecting their version attempting to fill in blanks.
We will respect that your past relationships are important.	Maintaining contact, treating relatives with respect, welcoming them, making unit approachable, involving parents in decisions, making visits happen, stopping other young people and staff being abusive about families.
We want you to keep positive links with the outside world.	Hobbies and clubs, being aware of what's in the community, contributing to the community, education within the community about who we are.

PRACTICE SUGGESTIONS
EDUCATION

It is essential to work in partnership with the school or college when making any plans for the improvement of a young person's educative experience. It is helpful to remember that during adolescence young people's preoccupations and developmental drives are likely to focus on:

- appearance

- behaviour

- achievement

- friendships

- sport

- leisure (Harter 1985).

We can key into these preoccupations, or even anxieties, by linking learning tasks with them. For example:

- an emphasis in some parts of the education process on the importance of self-care skills

- involvement with tasks that require collaboration with peers for their success

- leisure activities that may give the young person status in school

- deliberately shared activities with young people who are not in trouble and who have more personal resources.

It is helpful to work to the principle of using one strategy to join a number of aims across areas of intervention that will have ripple benefits across domains and will reduce effort for carers and workers. Involving the young person in discussion and negotiations about any difficulties they are experiencing, modelling collaborative problem-solving approach with parents and school staff is particularly important for adolescents. Dowling and Osborne (1985) provide many useful ideas for encouraging the positive involvement of the parents in their young person's schooling. Deliberate focused activities in school which concentrate on building self-esteem and celebrating achievement can be very helpful as described in another helpful text: *100 Ways to Enhance Self-Concept in the Classroom* (Cranfied and Wells 1994).

Encouraging the young person's interest in learning and school or college

1. Sometimes young people find it difficult to understand the point of school and the subjects learned. Modelling a notion that learning can be fun, and can have connection with the young person's individual aims in life, can offer a turning point for some young people. Thought needs to be given to ways in which numeracy and literacy can be encouraged as, not only will this offer encouragement to positive self-esteem, but also it will equip the young person in a fundamental way with ordinary life skills, for example, budgeting, applications for jobs, benefits. This can be done by linking the young person's natural enthusiasm with learning tasks, for example, in relation to maths: working out goal averages at football matches and places in the league.

2. There may be many opportunities to model a positive attitude to learning by, for example:

   (a) bringing young people books, talking about books

   (b) taking young people to libraries and historical places, e.g. castles, young person-oriented museums, bookshops

   (c) exploring the use of CD-ROMs and the internet

   (d) playing cards, darts and board games involving counting

   (e) letting them help work out mileage claims

   (f) encouraging them to use the local A–Z of street maps or road maps when driving to places.

3. Finding a particular area of responsibility (the more powerful if it combines with an interest) within the school or college setting can communicate positive expectations and may have surprisingly positive results for example, making a young person responsible for the artwork in the production of a school magazine or newspaper or involving him or her in the project in the local community stimulated from the school setting like a project in oral history.

4. When working with vulnerable young people model with them ways of:

   (a) nurturing their own well-being through attention to tiredness and hunger etc.

(b)   preparing resources to support themselves when undertaking difficult tasks

(c)   active reflection on performance.

5.   It may be that a critical turning point can be reached by the collaborative identification of a more suitable school or college placement for a young person who is experiencing particularly persistent problems. This can free the young person from a cycle of failure and begin to harness his or her capacities in a new way.

6.   Model alternative strategies for problem-solving in relation to school because many difficulties arise for young people in automatic, habitual, negative survival techniques which are not helpful in the school setting or in the care setting.

7.   Building on the young person's particular interest or achievement within the class timetable can be encouraged in school settings. Deliberately seeking to harness a young person's skills, for example, with drama, computers or art, can be linked with an important project involving the peer group at school. This can help the young person to develop a sense of belonging within the school setting. School staff can be involved in identifying a particular skill, talent or ability that can then be collaboratively nurtured between the school and the home setting.

8.   Help the young person to think and reflect about the successes at school so as to build confidence. Tune in to the young person's pattern of thinking about their abilities and capacities as many children who have had numerous separations and feel consequently powerless may have lost confidence in their capacities.

9.   Some young people will need extra support in the school setting and individual needs must be identified early on. Effective multidisciplinary assessments can be especially valuable here. Encouraging particular learning plans for young people who experience delays in their intellectual achievement, including flexibility of timetabling and content of work, can help to keep a young person within mainstream school setting.

10. Although the young person might adopt an attitude of not caring about school he or she is likely to feel keenly a sense of exclusion from 'normal' school activities and progress. Anything positive that the young person can be encouraged to identify about the school or college

as a place, education as a process or teachers as people can be used as a bridge back into schooling.

11. With adolescents it is essential that there is frequent consultation with them about their wishes, feelings, thoughts, ideas and strategies for planning aspects of their own lives, including schooling.

12. Encourage the young person's involvement in school trips and special activities, as well as holiday activity schemes, to enhance the young person's involvement with his or her peer group and to help with the identification of special interests or skills. Any opportunity for collaborative problem-solving in or out of the classroom setting can be extremely helpful in increasing self-efficacy: for example, shared problem-solving on a walking or climbing trip with the vulnerable young person involved in sharing responsibility with peers. Careful thought about the deliberate inclusion of young people with various kinds of disabilities and learning difficulties in such activities can be very important in promoting good peer relationships.

Encouraging a parent or carer environment that facilitates the young person's learning and school or college attendance

1. The educational and care professionals need to set out a clear learning journey for each young person that is shared with parents or carers. This will help in the setting out of reasonable expectations. The messages communicated from the important adults in the young person's life about the importance of schooling can be vital in setting the tone for the possibility of real achievement. Some parents will  need help in making and sustaining this link and this can be modelled by supportive professionals. Parents can be involved in the school setting in a number of ways, for example as helpers on school trips, or at break-times and this can be very important in building the key relationships which will sustain the vulnerable young person in the school setting. It can also have the secondary benefit of encouraging parents' confidence in communicating effectively with adults at school and therefore feeling more a part of their young person's education. School systems that harness parents' involvement in a genuine and consistent way are more likely to strengthen their commitment to keeping the young person within mainstream school setting.

2. Consider who supports the young person in school and think about the messages the parents, foster carers or residential workers want to convey to the young person about education and schooling and how they might do this. For example, conveying the message 'I am interested' by attendance at school meetings, asking the young person about their schooling, monitoring progress and collaboratively identifying aims and goals. Initiatives taken to involve parents at an early stage can offer them ideas as to how they might encourage the young person's school achievement by the use of activities at home.

3. Provide opportunities for parents to have access to learning materials that are being used with their young people to enable them to keep track of their young person's progress.

4. Young people are likely to need a private comfortable personal space or haven in which to study. Decorating and furnishing this together, even if it is only a corner of a room, with cushions and pictures and so on, can convey important messages about the value of the young person's education. Encouraging the young person's creativity and the presentation of work can require much persistence but have major benefits, for example, by purchasing even small items which make a major impact on the presentation of homework or projects. If the family is living in overcrowded or poor housing conditions then it may be very difficult for the young person to find space and peace in which to do homework. This issue can form part of a case to housing departments for a move to more suitable housing. In the mean time it may be helpful to see if anyone else in the extended family can offer the young person a peaceful space in which to work.

5. Look for somebody in the extended family or neighbourhood who could act as a homework mentor.

6. Encourage parents to attend parents' evenings and events within the school. Through this simple mechanism parents can not only establish a relationship with the individual teacher, but also gain an understanding of the patterns of formal learning which their young person is experiencing. Modelling parents' involvement in the school through support of the professionals involved can be helpful in establishing good communication and relationships with school staff. This should occur even if the young person is not living at home. Some parents have experienced difficulties in their own schooling, may be reluctant even to enter the school setting and may need considerable professional

support to begin to do this. Including parents wherever possible in the detail of assessment of their young person's difficulties can increase their knowledge and understanding of the nature of those difficulties and can harness them in supportive work to deal with the problems these difficulties cause for the young person.

7. There should be an assessment of the parents' own educational needs. Helping the parents to further their own education not only will be of benefit to them but also will have knock-on benefits for their young people. Community education and adult education organisations provide a variety of options of classes for adults.

8. Encourage parents to share and contribute their own skills within the school setting to send a positive message to the child, for example a parent who coaches the football team at school on a Saturday or the parent who makes costumes for a school performance.

Exploring opportunities in the wider environment to support this young person's education

1. Any opportunity for the young person to collaborate with other youngsters in the completion of tasks linked to school can help with a sense of inclusion. Ordinary community activities,  such as Guides or Scouts and swimming clubs can offer very important opportunities for young people who may be otherwise more isolated from their peer group in school. They can, furthermore, be particularly helpful for accommodated young people who may feel themselves set apart from their peers as their living circumstances are at odds with the family context of their classmates. The regular involvement of young people in local community clubs can, therefore, build a sense of social connectedness with the young person's peer group in the local community and begin to develop a sense of belonging.

2. If there is a particular teacher with whom the young person has developed a relationship of trust, then this teacher should be involved in planning meetings.

3. It can be useful, especially in work with vulnerable young people entering school, to identify a mentor to assist in getting a young person to school and supporting them through the day.

4.   Numerous initiatives have been generated by local communities in order to support young people in school settings. For example, groups of adults from particular racial groupings have become concerned about the number of young people from their own communities who appear not to be reaching their potential at school. Initiatives such as the individual linking of these supportive adults in the community with individual young people to support school progress can be profoundly helpful. The use of interested, committed individuals from the local community in supporting children who may be experiencing discrimination, for example, against children with disabilities or from different racial communities, can be an important way of counteracting prejudice.

5.   Many activity-based groups within the community can provide young people with opportunities for mastery and success in particular areas. For example, local groups which nurture young people's footballing or gymnastic skills can help with developing the young person's feeling of competence and these benefits can spill over into confidence in a school setting, particularly when these activities are undertaken with school peers. Shared activities in such a group can also build social competence, the development of empathy and responsiveness towards peers. The more the young person is involved in the local community and identifies with his or her peer group, the more beneficial this will be to establishing peer links and developing a sense of belonging. For example, community projects, celebrations or environmental initiatives can foster a sense of social responsibility and a sense of belonging to the school community.

6.   Within group settings such as residential homes, a range of strategies can be in place to encourage educational progress:

(a)   Link a teacher with a residential unit.

(b)   Create a culture of regular attendance and completion of work and the modelling of a sustained interest in progress and the identification of goals.

(c)   Communicate the message 'we care about you and want you to look after yourself' by a programme in relation to developing self-care, for example the purchasing of fashion items, saving for them by doing chores and sharing responsibility with other residents.

(d) Ensure that staff have detailed knowledge of the young person's curriculum.

(e) Establish a shared philosophy and commitment to sustaining the young person at school.

(f) Establish relationships with school staff, using school liaison groups, joint assessment teams and so on.

(g) Ensure education is considered in its broadest sense.

(h) Build annual personal profiles.

(i) Use group work.

(j) Give messages that education is valuable, that there are expectations, that there is interest in achievements, that education gives choices and control in life and that school is not just about education but has a social aspect.

(k) Demonstrate that education is lifelong, with staff modelling learning.

(l) Ensure that a consistent person attends parent's evenings.

(m) Create homework space and time by providing learning resources such as books, encyclopedias, CD-ROMs, access to the internet, Discovery TV.

(n) Ensure that staff have up-to-date knowledge about school systems.

(o) Provide trips with an educational slant.

(p) Get parents involved.

PRACTICE SUGGESTIONS
FRIENDSHIPS

When considering intervention within this domain it may be helpful to consider general peer relationships and specific friendships. It may be that a young person needs help with general peer relationships first before attention to particular friendships. Another young person might have many general acquaintances but no special friends. The starting point has to be the young person's perception of the situation: however many friends he or she may objectively appear to have, a young person can still feel lonely and it is that feeling that is important. So, before planning intervention take care to locate the root problem that is affecting friendships.

Helping the young person to develop the characteristics that help with making and keeping friends

1. If the young person appears to have problems with peer relationships in general then he or she may need help with social skills, as set out in the domain of Social Competencies.

2. Work to improve friendship skills by, for example, role play, modelling by carers and taking time to reflect with him or her on specific situations.

3. There may be strengths in other domains that can be used to help build upon this domain. For example, if the young person has a particular talent or interest he or she can be enrolled in a club or interest group in order to develop that talent, but also to enable contact with other young people who have similar interests. He or she can also be encouraged to pass expertise onto other young people, perhaps as part of a mentor scheme. If the young person is strong in the domain of academic performance he or she could be brought into a peer tutoring scheme and so on.

4. If the young person has difficulty with identifying special friends then spend time with him or her considering the peer network. It might be that the young person is trying to be friendly with people he or she has nothing in common with. Help young people to consider what they actually want from friendships and what they can offer as a friend. Do they have sufficient self-esteem to recognise that they have something to offer? Some young people adapt to having no friends by accepting the situation and isolating themselves from group activity, and therefore missing opportunities to change the situation.

5. If the young person describes friendships only on the basis of proximity, or in terms of doing things together, then help him or her to reflect upon other ways they can use friends, for sharing confidences and so on.

6. Young people who have experienced sexual abuse, for example, are often very frightened about their peers finding out. This could inhibit the sharing of confidences and make him or her seem aloof. Another

young person can react by talking inappropriately about the abuse and therefore alienating others. Give advice and help on sharing and hearing confidences. For example, the sharing of confidences usually involves a gradual increase in the level of intimacy. Help young people to identify how to match the level of confidence from a peer, perhaps to slightly increase it. Help them to develop a statement to use when the conversation is entering territory that they do not want to share, for example, 'I've had a lot of problems with my dad and it gets me upset to talk about him too much'.

7. The etiquette of true friendship is complicated; it involves keeping confidences, but knowing when it might be best to tell someone else if you are worried about a friend; learning how to handle gossip and talking behind someone's back; coping with jealousy and so on. The young person may need to identify an adult that they can seek advice from on such issues.

Encouraging a parent or carer environment that facilitates the development of friendship

1. As young people move into adolescence they should be in a position to take more responsibility for making their own arrangements for meeting with friends. However, the parent or carer environment is still influential. The approach to support parents and carers in providing the best environment for friendships depends upon the outcome required. The withdrawn young person  may need much more help with organising, arranging and getting together with friends. Perhaps other family members can be drawn in to help, perhaps a father, even if he does not live in the household. Young people who have plenty of friends, but friends with whom they get into trouble, might require more restriction and monitoring of their whereabouts. Parents and carers are entitled to decide that there are certain friends that they do not want to come to the house.

2. Parents may need support with other issues that help facilitate friendships, perhaps all the young person's friends have mobile phones: could the family and extended family be encouraged to pay the young person for some chores so that he or she can save up for one of their own?

3. Encourage the parent to talk to the young person about his or her friendships, to show interest in them and to respect them as important.

4. Sometimes it is assumed that adolescents turn to friends instead of parents and that their peers are more important to them. Although they may spend a lot of time with peers and they are valued, parents are still needed. It might not be so obvious that they are needed, but young people still require a secure family base from which to join peer activities. It might feel easier to parents to allow them to spend more and more time with friends, perhaps staying over frequently at other people's houses, but parents can be encouraged to make sure that the young person still has some time with them and that they have a base.

5. Parents and carers may need the opportunity to talk over how best to deal with disputes and problems in the young person's friendships.

Helping with the young person's current friendships

1. The young person who has not become involved in significant delinquent behaviour, but who has no friends, should benefit from an increase in peer contact and making friends.

2. The young person who is already involved in delinquent activity and who has a group of friends will benefit from a reduction in peer contact and the development of different friendships.

3. Younger children tend to make friendships on the basis of proximity and the young person's friendship skills may be immature. The challenge is to contrive ways of placing young people in proximity with young people without difficulties. School or college is the obvious setting for this, although all activities and clubs attended by young people in the community should be considered. Start by looking at mainstream activities for young people and then look at more specialist options.

4. If existing friendships are with other accommodated or troubled children, then finding ways to make the most of these friendships can be found. Increase the level of supervision by organising joint outings and activities.

5. Turner (1999) describes peer support initiatives for health promotion. Young people will often turn to peers for advice and information about

contraception, substance misuse, pregnancy and so on, but the friends don't always know how or what to advise. In peer support programmes young people are taught skills such as listening and basic counselling and are given information about services. Peer initiatives can improve knowledge and change attitudes as well as improving the self-esteem and self-efficacy of the helpers. The 'cascade' model of training new volunteers is effective. However, the volunteer helpers must be given ongoing support by a trained adult and such programmes require careful planning and ongoing support.

6.   When preparing young people for moving on to more independent living it is essential to help them to develop a support network in order to cope with adulthood. Work on developing a peer support network should begin well in advance of any move.

7.   Within residential units and foster care there are a whole range of possible factors that can promote friendship:

   (a)   Provide access to email and a telephone.

   (b)   Train young people to be befrienders.

   (c)   Teach social skills in relation to friendships, making use of the keyworker/advisory role.

   (d)   Make links with neighbourhood centres/youth clubs, perhaps make joint applications for funding to provide extra staff.

   (e)   Promote the maintenance of friendships.

   (f)   Work hard to help children sustain friendships on a practical level, for example, be prepared to taxi children to clubs and to meet friends, provide bus fares to go home and to the home neighbourhood and so on.

   (g)   Consider ways that protection can inhibit friendships, e.g. police checks of friends/families prior to sleepovers and so on. While this is a safeguard, the young person often finds this embarrassing, so enter into discussion with managers about how to develop a young-person-friendly policy of protection. Involve young people in the discussions.

   (h)   Encourage and support friendships with local community children, make links with the parents.

   (i)   Recognise the needs of young people who are being isolated by being accommodated.

(j)   Make activities fun and open for all.

(k)   Encourage friends to visit and create space and privacy for the young person's friends to visit.

(l)   Develop group work programmes on friendship.

(m) Help them keep in touch with old friends.

(n)   Help them to make new friends and make sure that staff get to know them.

(o)   Give the message that you want them to make friends, that the friends are valued, that they are likeable and have something to offer as a friend.

(p)   Manage the return of previous residents.

(q)   Ensure that staff are in control and will intervene when necessary.

(r)   Invite friends' parents to the unit and build relationships.

(s)   Encourage activities with friends and build on what they want to do.

(t)   Use befriending schemes.

(u)   Allow young people to just go out with friends, not necessarily on structured activities.

(v)   Be prepared to deal with unsuitable 'friends'.

PRACTICE SUGGESTIONS
TALENTS AND INTERESTS

It should be remembered that in considering the benefits *across* domains, talents and interests, especially those that bring them into contact with supportive adults and peers, can help the young person to settle within a new community and school or college setting.

If there is already an area of strength it will be important to capitalise on established skills. However, in the work with many young people, established talents and abilities may not be readily apparent and intervention should focus on how the young person's potential abilities can be explored.

The case studies at the end of this workbook illustrate the potential for using an ability or talent to support a healthy sense of identity in a young person who has experienced not only abuse, but also many separations and losses. It will be seen from the examples that some young people who avoid intimacy with caring adults, or who are ambivalent, can experience the support of adults over time in developing a set of talents. This, less obviously than direct attempts to bring the young person to accept caring overtures, can build young people's ability to depend healthily on those caring for them.

Therefore, this domain links closely with the notion of the young person being able to say 'I can' in relation to his or her own capacities. It also helps to build a sense of identity in exploring and establishing, not only competencies, but also a sense of identity rooted in a unique collection of attributes. In this way, the 'I can' contributes to the 'I am' or what can be seen as self-esteem.

Encouraging the young person in his or her particular talents and interests

1. Some adolescents have no idea even what activities they wish to try. A stalwart carer, parent or relative can be invaluable in persisting and trying out a whole range of different activities.

2. Some young people with disabilities can excel in particular areas and this may need persistent interest by at least one caring adult to discover and then support the talent or ability. This can begin to build a healthier sense of identity for a young person with a disability. For example, Derek has profound learning difficulties; however, he is a very expressive boy and has learned to use simple play figures to act out dramas and imaginative play. He recently chose this medium to begin to express some confusions and distress about the circumstances of his removal from home. His social worker and foster carer were able to harness this natural expressive ability in detailed emotional work on his life story.

3. A talent can give a vehicle for expressing feelings, for example:

    (a) cartoon drawing

    (b) computer skills

    (c) design or artistic skills.

4. A great deal of persistence may be required in finding a particular talent or ability in an individual young person. Because many young people have a natural lack of confidence, particularly if they have been ignored or discouraged, great tenacity can be required to communicate the belief in their ability by maintaining effort, even in the face of the young person's passivity and apparent diffidence.

5. Physical activities have the positive benefit of providing a natural discharge of tension and anxiety. This can help the young person to develop an awareness of his or her body and promote a sense of well-being. For example Mary, who was 13 and had a natural ability in running, needed the support of her coach to pace herself physically in order to make the most of her performance.

6. Confidence in a talent may allow the young person to begin to acknowledge for the first time fears about failures or gaps in knowledge, especially for a young person who is naturally defensive in his or her attitude.

7. At this stage new developmental capacities become apparent which can be harnessed in the enjoyment of a talent or interest and can be used to help young people value their skills for example, the ability to memorise details of a favourite sport team's scoring and progress through a league. This new capacity for memory can be developed and extended through the memorising of a dance or dance routine or songs. Similarly, young people can be encouraged to develop rational thinking, specifically linked between cause and effect, for example:

    'If I foul another player I will get sent off.'

    'If I practise hard I will be appreciated and succeed.'

    The key here is to select natural enthusiasm in the young person and link it deliberately with other skills and domains.

8. Although many adolescents will be at the stage of wanting to undertake activities with their peer group rather than with adults, many accommodated young people lack the social skills to make and sustain peer links even in activity-based groups. They may well need the support of an adult to

    (a) begin to believe they have any abilities

    (b) try out new activities

(c)   sustain interest and effort in the face of even small discouragements

(d)   manage the cooperation necessary to collaborate in group activities focused on a natural ability.

9.   Many adolescents will be reluctant to admit to an ability or diminish its importance for them unless deliberately encouraged by a supportive adult. Regular involvement of a caring adult alongside a young person can provide the basis for rebuilding trust with parents or connecting a young person with foster carers or residential staff.

10.   When a young person has lost skills because of many moves it is helpful to tune into what this young person has enjoyed or been good at in the past. It is useful to explore ways for him or her to be reconnected with this skill or activity, especially if it involves potential, for example a young person with ball skills being introduced to a new sport which can harness his or her natural ability.

Ensuring that the parent or carer environment supports the development of talents and interests

1.   There is a real opportunity for adults to learn from the young person in a particular area:

(a)   Teach me that dance.

(b)   Teach me that magic trick.

(c)   Show me how to make that kite.

(d)   Help me work the computer.

This can be a tremendous boost to the young person's self-esteem.

2.   Involvement in a favourite hobby or talent may be a useful focus for meaningful involvement of fathers with their children, including those in circumstances of marital or partner separation.

3.   It can be helpful, particularly when dealing with survival tactics appropriate to neglectful or abusive circumstances carried over into more nurturing environments, to emphasise young people's skill in protecting themselves by adapting their behaviour to survive. Some young people, for example, learn to 'read' adults' behaviour so as to avoid unpredictable violence or rejection and this skill can be harnessed to meet more constructive purposes in their relationships with more protective adults and/or peers. Other young people learn prematurely

to care for young siblings, denying their own needs for nurturing. The skill lies in the helping adults to label this learning in a positive way while encouraging young people to be aware of, and to communicate, their own needs. The way in which this is done can affirm young people's abilities while freeing them to focus on their own lives in a healthier fashion. For example, Zoe, 15, has always looked after her little brother and has many nurturing skills but neglects her own self-care. Her social worker was able to include her in the detailed plans for the care of her brother by foster carers while gradually including her in age-appropriate peer activities. She received many positive messages about her empathy with, and care of, her brother and was eventually able to delegate this to the foster carer.

4. Separated young people can still share enjoyable times with parents or relatives through shared activities that build a sense of family connection as well as individual competence. For example, Steven loves golf and his mother takes him to the driving range near to the foster carers when she visits. She collects pictures of his golfing heroes and the social worker has supported her by paying for basic lessons for Steven that his mother takes him to each week. Sarah's grandfather takes her to the home games of their local football team. He recently went to see her play in the school mixed team.

5. Some young people choose precisely the activity for which they are not obviously equipped, but this should not stop them taking part. For example, Shona particularly wanted to be good at gymnastics. Her coordination skills were poor, however, and her carers feared she would face disappointment. Through a close, cooperative link with the teacher in the local gymnastic class, her carers at first became 'helpers' supporting her to attend regularly. Because they have developed a knowledge of the exercises, they were then able to help her to practise at home and she soon surpassed their expectations, such was her determination. This interest provided a shared activity that was powerful in building her gradual attachment to her carers.

6. Parents may need support to believe in their own abilities to help their young person to develop a talent or a skill. For example, if they have had poor experiences of play in their own childhood they may be at a loss as to how to create opportunities for play for their young person. It may well be constructive to support parents individually or in groups to enjoy play opportunities for themselves and to rediscover or find out for the first time their own skills and capacities.

7.   Working with parents' own talents, abilities and strengths has many advantages as it models confidence and enjoyment for the young person. For example, Kelly's mother, Susan, rediscovered her dance skills through going to a local dance class and realised she could teach her daughter, who also has a natural ability. Mother and daughter now regularly attend classes together, an activity that they both enjoy.

Drawing upon opportunities in the wider community to nurture the young person's talents and interests

1.   It is helpful to remember that some young people need more assistance than others at this stage to take part in a shared group activity involving a skill or an ability. Billy, who tended to lash out when frustrated, needed the support of his uncle to sustain attendance at the football club. His uncle's involvement in the club and regular encouragement made it possible for Billy to sustain an activity for the first time. Paula's adolescent foster sister, Laura, is a medal and cup winner in the drum majorettes and Paula loves to go to the sessions with Laura and in fact won her own first medal recently. Gareth has an interest and ability in modern dance but is teased about this at school. His male foster carer actively supports him and encourages him to practise at home. His achievements are celebrated in the foster home with photographs, videos and certificates that have been framed by the carers and are on the walls in the sitting room.

2.   Make a careful assessment of the young person's existing abilities to develop and sustain his or her chosen activity in order to gauge what level of support is likely to be needed to promote mastery and the development of necessary skills. For example, Joe, aged 13, has natural skills in playing football but is frequently rejected by his peers because he is so impulsive. His uncle has been organising games with a few of Joe's local peers and helping Joe to learn to cooperate more effectively. When Sarah feels uncertain, she will withdraw from her swimming class and claim that she is ill. Her older foster sister, who is a good swimmer, identifies when this is about to happen and gently encourages Sarah.

Paul is 15 and very passive in the residential unit. His keyworker has embarked on a series of 'taster' sessions for different activities and they have discovered that Paul has a natural artistic ability. He has begun to attend a local class in sculpture but regularly destroys his figures and needs the consistent encouragement of his worker to attend.

Ryan is 14 and very reluctant to express any feelings about his life circumstances. His carers have involved him in a local drama club where he has become very involved in a small play working cooperatively for the first time with other young people.

Smitha, who is 12 and from an Indian family, has many confusions about her identity. Her carers have enrolled her in an Indian dance class where she meets adults from her own community and is learning about her own culture and traditions with the support of the dance teacher. She recently performed with the group at the local Mela Festival.

Scott, 15, has a fascination for cars and has been involved in 'taking and driving away' offences. His residential worker has linked him with a local group that teaches vulnerable young people mechanic skills. This group includes a local police officer and this link has gradually challenged Scott's prejudice and aggression towards the police.

3. A talent or hobby can offer a link with a different group of peers, thereby opening up social networks for accommodated young people, for example:

    (a) joining a drama group in the local community

    (b) exploring a musical interest by joining a group either in the community or from a school base

    (c) developing skills such as running, climbing, ball skills or gymnastics.

4. Shared interests at this age and stage can form a common basis of friendship either in school or in an interest group in the community, for example Guides, Venture Scouts, etc. This can be all the more important if the interest is a solitary one, such as computing.

5. Deliberate involvement in a club or group activity within the community, for example, football or darts, can have the following advantages:

    (a) attune the young person to traditional activities within his or her culture, for example, Indian dance

    (b)   offer an access to a base for the attainment and refinement of skills which are emergent

    (c)   provide links with other young people with similar interests

    (d)   if a young person is placed in accommodation with others with similar problems, change the emphasis of some aspects of the young person's social experience by placing him or her in an activity with more able peers in other community settings.

6. Talents which offer a chance of a position of responsibility in any group activity can promote self-esteem and confidence in social situations. For example, Kirsty, with the support of her singing teacher, took responsibility for making the accommodation arrangement for her singing group who were going on a local tour. In one locality the young people helped to set up a football coaching scheme that involved the local police, the young people and the police involved developed good relationships.

7. Young people from minority cultures can find a secure base in activities linked with their own cultural heritage, for example dance or key position in religious observance to rituals. Finding an adult to act as a mentor from the young person's natural networks in the community is particularly important here.

8. In residential units, the culture of the setting communicates many subtle messages to young people as to their potential and uniqueness in the eyes of caring adults. It can be helpful to review the practices so as to avoid using a merely problem-focused approach. The search for unique apparent or potential talents and abilities can begin from the point of admission. Planning strategies to pursue these areas on a persistent basis models a positive approach and a belief in potential. Engaging in activities alongside each young person provides many opportunities for developing trust and communicating commitment.

9. Some may require intensive support in developing any confidence that they may have skills or talents, such may have been the strength of feelings of powerlessness in the face of abuse or neglect or even repeated unpredicted transitions or separations. Setting aside time on a regular predictable basis to pursue talents and interests is a powerful message in itself though many young people will test the workers' seriousness and reliability, such has been their experience of failure and disappointment. For example, May would suddenly disappear from the

unit when her keyworker was arriving to take her to her evening class. It was only after several weeks of persistence that the apparent dismissive attitude in Mary changed and she began to attend regularly and to enjoy the activities. Andy, 14, who has cerebral palsy, had very poor self-esteem and would produce reasons for not going to the computer class. After many an early hiccup in his commitment he has produced, some months later, an Alternative Guide to his residential school harnessing his new skills and his wry sense of humour. Incidentally, his teachers have noticed a new enthusiasm for learning over the past years as he is learning to adapt these new skills to the school setting.

10. A range of strategies can be put in place within units to help encourage a culture that nurtures talents and interests:

   (a)   Use group work to provide a wide range of taster experiences.

   (b)   Offer the choice to participate in activities (sometimes without an audience), like outward-bound activities, arts and crafts, aromatherapy, sports, ice-skating, bowling, going for a meal, to see a play, on a holiday, playing games, quizzes and self-care activities, for example 'make-overs'.

   (c)   Use activities whereby young people have to help each other, such as teamwork, team-building.

   (d)   Tackle 'learned helplessness' via shared responsibilities, involving young people in activities or games, before they have had a chance to worry about it, reinforce positives and repeating activities.

   (e)   Offer praise and recognition.

   (f)   Ask and listen to what they like, as opposed to what they are good at.

   (g)   Interests and pursuits should not be curtailed as a sanction.

   (h)   Help their parents to promote young people's talents.

   (i)   Recognise that all young people give up on things and this should not stop them from going on to try further activities.

   (j)   Provide finance for talent and interests: do not allow cost to be a hurdle to participation.

   (k)   Arrange for continuity of staff to accompany a young person to an activity.

(l)   Have facilities available, like cameras and cassette recorders, so the young people can record things, games, crafts and other material resources.

(m) Encourage and support involvement in community activities.

(n)   Find imaginative ways of tackling racism, bullying and sexism and do not allow traditional roles to stop activities such as boys cooking or girls playing football.

(o)   Be positive, not so much about how much is achieved but what young people get out of it.

(p)   Do not make throwaway comments or show insensitivity by laughing at young people.

(q)   Respect individuality.

(r)   Build on small components to achievement.

(s)   Keep close communication between residential and field social workers.

(t)   Allow staff time to use their talents and recognise their interests or abilities.

(u)   Keep up to date with knowledge of resources.

PRACTICE SUGGESTIONS
POSITIVE VALUES

Helping this young person develop moral reasoning and to understand his or her own feelings and empathise with those of people close to them

1.   Some young people whose emotional life has been very deprived may be operating at a much younger level in this domain. You may want to draw on suggestions from the *School Years* workbook in these cases.

2. A technique of using 'dilemma discussion groups' has been shown to be a successful way to raise adolescent levels of moral reasoning (Goldstein 1999). A full description of the technique is beyond the scope of these workbooks; however, the principles could be applied to a range of group settings, perhaps using the dilemma provided. Briefly, the technique involves holding discussions with a group of young people operating at different levels of moral reasoning. The group leaders should be familiar with the different levels of reasoning. Their role is to encourage the young people to explain the underlying reasoning for their responses to different moral dilemmas, preferably as real to life as possible. They then encourage debate among young people at different levels. The leaders do not express a view as to what is the right or wrong answer, but aim to provide an environment of openness and trust in which young people can themselves work out what is 'good'.

3. Real situations in which the young person has been in trouble can be used as a basis for a discussion in which the focus in mainly upon the *reasoning* behind an action. If a young person has been caught stealing, for example, he or she can be asked questions such as:

    (a)   What if everybody stole what they wanted?

    (b)   What if no one stole things?

    (c)   What if your best friend took something of yours?

    (d)   What if someone you don't like took something of yours?

    (e)   How do you think people can get things without stealing?, and so on.

4. The activities described for school-age children might be applicable for some younger adolescents who show problems with empathy (see *School Years* workbook).

5. It is through relationships with others that young people begin to develop an understanding of their own and others' feelings. Ensure that there is at least one person in the young person's life who has the interest and the time to listen to him or her, explore feelings and demonstrate respect and empathy for the young person.

6. Adolescents should be given as many opportunities for choice as possible. If their wishes and feelings have been consistently ignored or overridden they are likely to have difficulty with identifying their own true preferences. The more that they are actively involved in any discussions, plans and decisions the better.

Encouraging the young person to help others

1. The parent or carer should be encouraged to recognise, accept and praise any verbal offers of help or apparent attempts to help. Adolescents should be able to help in many ways. First, they should be increasingly encouraged to take personal responsibility for self-care, ensuring that their own clothes are washed and ironed and keeping their own living space reasonably clean and tidy. Second, they should be expected to help with general household chores. Finally, they should be increasingly able to anticipate what may be needed in the way of help. A clear system of rewards may be helpful here.

2. In chaotic households it may be difficult to organise chores for the adolescent if there is no expectation for regular household activities to be carried out. In other households it is considered appropriate only for girls to be asked to help. Consider involving male and female adolescents in discussions with parents about expectations of household cleanliness. Indeed the whole family can be allocated different tasks.

3. When there is no appropriate support for a young person's helping behaviour in the home, and the likelihood of this changing is minimal, then involve the young person in a discussion about whether there are members of the extended family who need help, especially grandparents, or relatives with young children. There is evidence that helping with younger children can encourage the development of resilience in older children.

Encouraging the young person to show comforting, sharing and more general prosocial behaviour

1. The ideal way for young people to learn positive behaviour is by imitation. All interactions with the young person should therefore model caring and comforting. Again the parent or carer has to be the

main resource here. Parents may need advice and support to actively encourage comforting and sharing behaviour between siblings and the young person and other young people.

2.   Young people should be given clear rules and boundaries about behaviour towards others and any signs of cruelty, unkindness or hurting to other young people or adults should be stopped.

3.   Any spontaneous act of sharing or kindness should be praised and reinforced. Parents may need advice on how best to do this.

4.   Contact with pets and animals can help with the development of kindness. If it is not appropriate for there to be a pet in the household, there may be opportunities for young people to help with a relative or neighbour's pet, for example they can be encouraged to offer to walk a neighbour's dog.

5.   If a young person is showing active signs of cruelty to others then his or her behaviour will require a high level of monitoring by skilled staff who can intervene as quickly as possible with firm and clear messages against harm to others. All in the young person's network need to work together to give consistent and clear messages about kindness to others.

6.   Young people need to have contact with their peers in order to learn about cooperative activities. School or college are the obvious places for the encouragement of cooperation. Ensure that the young person has access to some form of formal or informal contact with other young people that is supervised by an adult skilled in facilitating cooperative activities. Young people can be referred to one of the many group work programmes set up to involve a range of activities that require cooperation. Outdoor activity programmes are often very popular with adolescents. When involving young people in group work take time before they join the group to discuss the values of the group with them so that they are prepared for, and understand, the requirements of mutual respect, confidentiality and so on.

7.   Young people live up to the attributions ascribed to them, so whenever appropriate they need to hear that they are good and kind: 'That was kind of you to…'

8.   Find community-based schemes that promote responsibility and empathy, for example, local clean-up river campaigns, anti-litter drives,

sponsored walks, charity collections and so on. Wherever possible involve the young person in mainstream community activities.

9. Adolescents can be involved in buddying schemes with younger children, to help them with schoolwork, or with other activities of mutual interest.

10. Responsible behaviour must be expected of young people. Sometimes professionals are so aware of the reasons behind an adolescent's difficult behaviour that they are prepared to overlook antisocial behaviour. However, because prosocial values are strongly associated with better outcomes it is essential that a programme be put in place that is built upon an expectation that the young person can overcome his or her previous problems.

11. Within group settings such as residential homes for young people, it is the whole ethos that contributes to the development of prosocial values in adolescents. A range of factors have to be put in place to create a setting that fosters mutual respect, empathy and sharing, including:

    (a) model and demonstrate positive values with young people and colleagues

    (b) listen with respect to their beliefs and values

    (c) recognise diversity

    (d) create a climate which encourages debate about values

    (e) create a forum for debate about values

    (f) match mission by practice

    (g) prepare to concede in debate and discussion with young people

    (h) allow for 'safe' risk-taking

    (i) create a shared ethos

    (j) actively look for and reward any instances of prosocial behaviour

    (k) use humour

    (l) be sincere in relationships

    (m) create small group settings

    (n) ensure that the physical environment is of high quality and involves the young person in the design and choice of furnishings

    (o) ensure consistency and continuity of staffing levels.

PRACTICE SUGGESTIONS
SOCIAL COMPETENCIES

A considerable number of resources are available to help with the promotion of social competencies in school-age children, many of them designed for use in schools. The 'Promoting Social Competence' project has compiled a database of such resources (Promoting Social Competence 1999).

Some examples of programmes that might be helpful are described below.

Peterson and Gannoni's *Stop Think Do* which uses traffic light symbols as a motif within a range of activities aimed at encouraging young people to stop and think of options rather than acting on impulse (Peterson and Gannoni 1992).

Kreidler's *Creative Conflict Resolution* contains more than 200 simple activities aimed at teaching children strategies for dealing with problems in social interaction. Designed primarily for classroom use, many of the activities could be adapted for use in other group settings, or on a one-to-one basis (Kreidler 1984).

Spence's *Social Skills Training* is again designed for use in schools, but contains a range of questionnaires and checklists for children and teachers on problems of social situations, social skills and so on. There is a photocopiable resource book which has paper-and-pencil task sheets to help children consider alternative ways of responding (Spence 1995).

Goldstein's *Prepare Curriculum* describes a whole range of activities for teaching prosocial and social competence skills. It sets out the research base for different approaches and gives detailed descriptions of individual and group programmes (Goldstein 1999).

Wheal's *Positive Approaches for Working with Young People* is aimed specifically at those working with adolescents and sets out suggestions for working with parents, successful communication and encouraging positive behaviour and includes ideas on education, health, equality and the law in the UK (Wheal 1998).

Before looking at suggestions for each of the aspects, we will set out an overall framework for considering social competence problems.

Smith and Carlson (1997) have brought together much useful information about children's coping with stress. In summary, they describe coping as involving four steps:

1. Appraisal of the meaning of the event, whether it is stressful and whether it might be controllable.

2. Selecting a coping strategy that is appropriate to the circumstances.

3. Carrying out the coping strategy.

4. Evaluating whether the coping strategy has been successful.

Some stressful situations are malleable and to some extent controllable. Other stressors are uncontrollable. When stressors are malleable it is better to use the active (or 'primary') problem-focused coping strategies such as gaining information or actually changing the stressor. When the situation is uncontrollable then it is better to use the passive (or 'secondary') emotion-focused strategies such as changing the way you think about the stressor or adapting to it. Therefore the accuracy of attributions made about events can affect choice of coping strategy and the likelihood of success. Put simply the choice is between changing the events or changing how you think and feel about the events.

Adolescents have been shown to have the capacity to use both problem-focused and emotion-focused coping strategies. Emotion-focused strategies, in particular, require maturity in being able to change one's outlook and regulating emotions. A range of factors can influence the choice and success of coping strategy. To use a problem-focused strategy young people must believe that they can have an impact on the stressor; they need a good sense of self-efficacy. They also need problem-solving skills and the social skills to enlist social support. Economic resources can help 'buy' the emotion-focused strategies of distraction, such as entertainment.

The key to developing effective intervention then is to assess accurately where the young person's problem with social competence lies in the chain of coping as shown in Figure 9.1.

APPRAISAL

Is this event likely to be stressful?

(Requires ability to assess whether an event is likely to affect well-being)

↓

Is this event in any way under my control?

↓

(Requires accurate attributions and self-efficacy)

CHOICE OF COPING STRATEGY

What can I do about this event?

(Requires a range of strategies and ability to match strategy to problem)

PROBLEM-FOCUSED

Have I strategies I can use?
(Requires coping resources such as
problem-solving skills)

Can I put these strategies into action?
(Requires self-efficacy and self-esteem)

EMOTION-FOCUSED

Can I change the way I
think about this event?
(Requires self-efficacy and self-esteem)

Can I change the way I
feel about this event?
(Requires emotional support, family or
social support)

↓

CARRYING OUT THE STRATEGY

(Requires confidence, courage and expectation of success)

↓

EVALUATING THE STRATEGY

(Requires ability to reflect and learn from experience)

Figure 9.1 The chain of coping that enables successful social competence

For example, a young person who lacks social competence may not relate well to adults because she consistently wrongly appraises adults as being critical. She needs to learn strategies of assessing an adult who is talking to her, paying attention to the facial expressions, listening to what the adult is saying and so on.

Another young person might accurately appraise that an adult is not being critical, but finds it stressful because he does not feel that he has the interpersonal skills to respond properly, he feels shy or tongue-tied and that he has no control over the situation. He needs to learn simple strategies of engaging with adults. Role play can be an ideal way to teach a young person such skills and thereby to boost self-efficacy.

Another young person might choose emotion-led strategies such as thinking 'It doesn't matter what that adult says, only my friends matter', 'I don't care if I am criticised', 'I don't like her so it doesn't matter if she is critical'. She might also benefit from learning more problem-focused strategies of how to respond to adults.

Another might consistently storm out of the room when asked to help out at home. This leads to more arguments and conflict. What he does not realise is that his strategy is not effective, because he considers only the short-term benefit of avoiding the work. He might benefit from looking at the longer-term outcome (family tension and ongoing anger) and thinking of other options, for example, negotiating an agreed set of chores.

Helping the young person to develop the personal characteristics that help with social competence

AUTONOMY

Adolescents are often compared to toddlers in their quest for autonomy. Parents may need information and reassurance about this stage of development. The parent or carer and young person could be involved in a joint discussion about the ways in which autonomy can be encouraged appropriately. This could include:

- agreeing a time for return in the evening
- arranging contingency plans if the young person is going to be late (phoning home)
- involving him or her in all decision-making processes as far as possible
- seeking his or her opinion on a matters affecting him or her

- ensuring that he or she has access to money of their own, possibly by payment for chores, to spend as he or she wishes

- supporting him or her to make arrangements to meet with friends

- giving him or her responsibilities.

SELF-CONTROL/PROBLEM-SOLVING

Young people need to learn a range of problem-solving skills if they are to engage in problem-focused coping strategies for social situations. In the commercially existing programmes for teaching social competencies a number of themes and techniques emerge that can be adapted:

1. Teaching adolescents to stop and think before acting – thinking can be encouraged in discussion, in groups or by using written vignettes that the young person is asked to consider.

2. Demonstrating alternative ways of reacting and then encouraging role play of situations that are directly relevant to the young person.

3. Taking a problem situation and helping the young person to identify the *thoughts* and *feelings* that the situation evoked. Looking at the links between the thoughts and feelings, and helping the young person to replace the thoughts with different thoughts. For example, if the young person lends a friend a CD and the friend loses it he could think 'He didn't look after it because he can't really be bothered with me' and feel hurt and rejected. Instead he could think 'It's quite easy to lose things, I've lost CDs myself'.

4. Group-based cognitive-behavioural programmes are effective for teaching interaction with friends, sensitivity to others and resisting peer presure as well as the skills of communicating clearly, problem-solving and self-control (Smith and Carlson 1997).

5. Wheal (1998) suggests some principles when trying to promote positive behaviour:

   (a) be supportive

   (b) keep it impersonal

   (c) be specific about the problem

   (d) handle problems one at a time

   (e) keep an open mind

   (f) specify the requirements

(g)   don't rush for a solution

(h)   agree actions and dates

(i)   always set a review date

(j)   praise good behaviour

(k)   handle complaints.

7.   Wheal (1998) describes the La Vigna model for tackling antisocial
behaviour (LaVigna and Donellan 1986) that suggests considering four
avenues for intervention:

(a)   Environment change – in which the focus is on changing the
environment so that appropriate behaviour is encouraged. This
might include making changes in the physical environment, for
example, in premises, crowding, noise and so on. It might involve
bringing more structure into their use of time, improving the
quality of relationships and allowing young people a forum for
expressing their views and it might mean tackling issues of health
and confidence.

(b)   Teaching new skills – in which the focus is on analysing the intent
of the behaviour and teaching different means to an end. Young
people's antisocial behaviour is often a result of unhelpful coping
strategies that have been learnt, and often hinge on problems of
communication. Young people can be taught better communication
skills, for example with assertiveness training.

(c)   Reinforcement – in which the focus is on increasing and
reinforcing positive behaviour, rather than inadvertently
reinforcing bad behaviour by allowing it to gain the young person
attention.

(d)   Reactive strategies – in which the focus is upon immediate
strategies for dealing with inappropriate behaviour as it occurs.
These might include anticipating problems within groups and
intervening promptly, listening to the message the young person is
conveying, removing the young person from a tense situation and
so on.

TEMPERAMENT

Having a positive easy temperament is a major factor in promoting resilience. For a
young person with a less easy temperament the most effective care is that which

meshes with the young person. If a parent withdraws from a difficult young person and is critical, then the young person is likely to become even more difficult. If looking for alternative full-time carers or mentors, then attention has to be paid to the 'fit' between the adult and young person's temperament. For example, some adolescents prefer to spend time alone when upset, others find it helpful to talk to an adult, others to talk to a friend, others need physical comfort. Young people can be encouraged to reflect upon their own temperamental requirements and to discuss how best to obtain support when it is needed.

SELF-EFFICACY

1. Young people who have been neglected or abused frequently develop attributions for events as out of their control, likely to remain negative and as being global. This can make them very reluctant to try new tasks, because they believe that they will fail. The experience of positive events, such as an enjoyable outing, the concentrated attention of a liked adult and so on, can help to change this view that good things will not happen to them.

2. The young person has to be encouraged to try tasks at which he or she can succeed. This requires skill on behalf of the helper to manipulate situations so that the young person tries something almost before realising it. Outdoor activities are ideal for this.

3. The young person also then needs to learn that some tasks are not within his or her range and that this is not their fault. For example, sporting activities can be useful here; a young person can, through sport, learn that practice can lead to improvement. The coach can also provide a role model of someone who is good at the sport, but recognises that he or she does not have the right build and skill to be an Olympic contender.

ATTENTION

By adolescence young people should be able to direct and focus their attention in academic and social situations. Try to find a member of the young person's network or a mentor who is prepared to spend some concentrated time with the young person on a regular occasion. A number of activities can be suggested:

1. Encourage and reward the young person for looking at you when you talk to him or her.

2. Engage the young person's attention and talk to him or her about things that interest him or her, all the while praising him or her for listening.

3. Find an activity that he or she expresses an interest in and encourage them to find out more about that activity and take part in it.

4. Encourage attention by watching a video with the young person and asking questions about what he or she anticipates will happen next. Make bets on the outcome; point out details the young person may not have noticed.

5. Adults often complain that young people will concentrate only on computer games. Perhaps this could be capitalised upon by enlisting them to help with a project that requires the seeking of information from a CD-ROM or the internet.

6. Make sure that you listen to things that young people try to tell you, show that you are interested in hearing what they have to say, ask them further questions about what they are telling you, draw other members of the family into the conversation.

7. Ensure that school or college work tasks are broken down into manageable chunks, and gradually increase the size of the chunks.

SENSE OF PURPOSE AND FUTURE

If young people have no hope that they have a positive future, they can develop a pattern of aggressive, impulsive, risky or self-destructive behaviour (Garbarino 1999). Warnings about how they might be damaging their prospects will have no impact on young people who do not believe they have prospects. Intervention should instead focus on helping to widen their options for the future, concentrating on further education, training, helping them to develop satisfying friendships and relationships, encouraging them to imagine themselves in a few years time and so on.

Helping the parent or carer to provide an environment that encourages social competence

1. The most successful social competence interventions focus on all ecological levels. As well as helping the young person to learn social skills and to develop self-efficacy, intervention should aim to create a home environment that fosters good interpersonal skills (Masten and Coatsworth 1998). Work with the parent or carer to devise a list of

social competencies that they would like to see their young person develop. Help them to develop strategies, based upon reward, for their encouragement. For example, praise for responding quickly when spoken to or for helping out in the home.

2.   Authoritative parenting incorporates both warmth and consistent boundaries. Parents may well benefit from the opportunity to attend a parenting group where they can share their experiences with others and consider different ways of encouraging social competence in their children. By adolescence young people still require boundaries, but also need room to negotiate those boundaries. They need explanations for rules and sanctions that make sense to them. For example, they need to know that when a parent sets a time for them to return at night it is because they care about them and worry about them.

3.   When parents themselves lack social competence and perhaps condone their children's behaviour, then look for an alternative role model for the young person, for example a member of the extended family, a mentor, volunteer, keyworker, teacher and so on.

Helping the young person to develop competence in a wider social environment

1.   Ensure that the young person has access to and knows how to make use of social support, either informal (friends, extended family) or formal (mentors, social workers, teachers, club leaders).

2.   Encourage the community to provide and develop local projects for teenagers.

3.   Encourage social interaction, open communication in a warm and accepting environment.

4.   Model conflict resolution for example by calling family conferences.

5.   Involve the young person in reviews and meetings; involve the young person in setting the agenda, choosing the venue for pieces of work and so on. Meaningful rather than token involvement might require coaching the young person in techniques for communicating in formal meetings. Wherever possible the young person should

be encouraged to produce his or her own reports, either in writing, or by dictation.

6. Encourage and facilitate the young person to participate in drawing up rules and sanctions in a number of different settings.

7. Refer to appropriate group work programmes, preferably within mainstream settings.

8. Make sure young people know they have choices.

9. Within group settings such as residential homes, a range of strategies can be in place to encourage social competencies.

   (a) A consistent staff group rather than a string of temporary workers.

   (b) Shared rules for social engagement that apply to staff and young people.

   (c) Staff who will give reliable support.

   (d) Staff who model what can and cannot be done, for example asking for help is a skill that can be learned by observation.

   (e) Encouragement for the young people to take ownership of their environment.

   (f) Opportunities for young people to 'make things right' if there is a problem.

   (g) Strategies to put things right quickly when there is a problem.

   (h) Plans that are seen through, for example, the implementation of a behavioural strategy for controlling antisocial behaviour.

   (i) Continuous assessment and review.

   (j) Encouragement for young people to participate fully in reviews and to give their feedback.

   (k) A degree of flexibility in development of rules and sanctions.

   (l) Provision of information for young people about their options and who they can turn to both inside and outside the unit.

   (m) Access to materials and resources for learning social competencies.

   (n) Promotion of positive relationships by inviting friends, family members and others to the unit.

10

Case Studies

ALISON, AGED 13

Vulnerabilities and adversities

Alison was placed with adopters together with her two younger sisters at 11 years old. She had a history of sexually abusive treatment by her stepfather and lengthy profound emotional neglect. She had an ambivalent pattern of attachment and was particularly disdainful towards and avoidant of her male carer. She had great difficulty making secure attachments and had no friendship skills. Her self-esteem was very low and she had no confidence in her abilities or potential.

Interventions

SECURE BASE

Her adopters were, and still are, profoundly committed to her but at times despaired of her ability to make close relationships and were at a loss as to how to help her.

EDUCATION AND TALENTS AND INTERESTS

A music teacher at school discovered that she had a lovely singing voice and selected herself as Alison's supporter in the school setting. She and Alison's adoptive parents encouraged her gently but consistently to nurture her singing ability. She became part of a group of talented young people who rehearsed, travelled and performed together. She gradually gained confidence and self-esteem. She learned, through her singing, skills of presentation; her concentration improved and she eventually coped with support with the challenges of solo performance. She became a valued member of the group and had a real place in the school as a young person with a unique talent. This, in turn, gave her a place in the community.

Alison was at considerable risk of premature sexual relationships because of her sexualised behaviour learned from the abusive experiences. Her singing teacher was much younger than her adoptive parents and therefore more readily available as a role model. She believed profoundly in Alison's potential and set reasonable but high expectations of her. Alison made two sound friendships with other girls who are still available to her as a young adult.

She was supported through college by her carers and has since established a relationship with a young man and they now have a child. Much to her carers' surprise and delight, she is a loving mother who takes excellent care of her little daughter. She still belongs to a singing group, which she enjoys.

Messages

The sensitive attention and involvement of her teacher in identifying and nurturing Alison's singing talent has been a vital component of Alison's developing confidence and self-esteem. While support to her carers has been central in helping them to withstand her avoidance of close attachments, their commitment has allowed Alison to learn from their care of *her*, the skills in nurturing evident in her empathy towards and care of her own child.

The value of her *talent* has been continually reinforced in her local school and wider community offering her a sense of belonging. Her relationship with her carers has now strengthened. She is only recently able to reflect openly with them on her past and her early memories which she vehemently resisted in her adolescence.

To set 'reasonable but high expectations' requires sensitive attunement in the adults to current attainment and potential. The link between her carers and teacher provided a network of support which gradually extended to include her new friendships.

TOM, AGED 15

Vulnerabilities and adversities

- Tom had been blamed for the death of his mother and had very low self-esteem. He experienced emotional abuse in the form of rejection, scapegoating and isolation from his family.

- He had repeated experiences of abrupt separations as a result of failed placements with a series of ambivalent family members. These separations had interrupted the maturational tasks of adolescence and he had an ambivalent pattern of attachment, showing little trust in adults.

- He appeared to have no language with which to express his feelings and instead communicated with sustained aggressive behaviour.

- His schooling was disrupted by poor attendance and characterised by under-achievement. Ejection from mainstream schooling had coincided with a placement change.

- His friendships were based on shared offending behaviour.

- He had lost any links with a community.

Resilience and protective factors

- Tom had a sense of humour.

- Some family members were at a loss but still remained tentatively in touch.

- There was a committed, persistent professional team and good communication between the workers.

- Positive use had been made of a secure care option and there was an experienced residential team with a repertoire of tested behaviour management skills.

- Educational and care resources were closely linked.

Intervention

SECURE BASE

- There was consultation with Tom about his wishes for contact and strategies were put in place for re-negotiating family links.

- Active support was provided by unit staff and timeous meetings were held.

- A previous link with a youth support worker from the community was resumed in anticipation of Tom's ultimate transition to independence.

EDUCATION

- There was detailed, joint planning of the use of the special educational resource and ongoing communication within the working team.

- Tom's progress was regularly reviewed.

- He was shown acceptance but given clear behavioural boundaries.

- He was provided with educational opportunities that allowed him to experience success and mastery.

TALENTS AND ABILITIES

- He was offered a place on a local voluntary project that used training in car maintenance to develop mechanical skills and group co-operation.

SOCIAL COMPETENCIES

- A criminal justice worker was involved to work on problem-solving skills combined with anger management strategies.

- Active work was carried out to help Tom make sense of the past and to help him gain insight into his current attributions in relation to life events.

Messages

- Communication between members of the working team was essential for consistency of the messages provided to Tom.

- The modelling of alternative behaviour and solutions to problems in an atmosphere of basic acceptance was vital.

- The confidence shown by the working team communicated the belief in the possibility of sustained change.

- A small number of carefully planned interventions in one domain can result in gains across into other domains, for example, work on group-cooperation helped to encourage progress in problem-solving skills.

Moral Reasoning Stages

The most famous example used to assess moral reasoning is that of Kohlberg (1969, p.379).

> In Europe, a woman was near death from a very bad disease, a special kind of cancer. There was one drug that the doctors thought might save her. It was a form of radium that a druggist in the same town had recently discovered. The drug was expensive to make, but the druggist was charging ten times what the drug cost him to make. He paid $200 for the radium and charged $2000 for a small dose of the drug. The sick woman's husband, Heinz, went to everyone he knew to borrow the money, but he could only get together about $1000, which was half of what it cost. He told the druggist that his wife was dying, and asked him to sell it cheaper or let him pay later. But the druggist said, 'No, I discovered the drug and I'm going to make money from it.' Heinz got desperate and broke into the man's store to steal the drug for his wife.
>
> Should the husband have done that? Was it right or wrong?

It is the reasons given for the answer that were more interesting to Kohlberg than the actual answer. Table A.1 shows the stages of reasoning he found. In summary the reasons given fall into one of three broad categories (Steinberg 1993): preconventional, conventional or postconventional.

Preconventional level

Typical of younger children, up to the age of about 9, this level of reasoning focuses on rewards and punishments. There is no reference to societal rules or conventions. Justifications for actions are based upon meeting one's own interests and letting others do the same. Examples of responses at this stage (from Steinberg 1993) would be that it would be right to steal the drug 'because people would have been angry with him if he let his wife die' or that he would be wrong to because he would be put in prison.

Conventional level

This level is demonstrated from middle childhood and into adolescence and often beyond into adulthood. The focus here is more upon how others, especially significant others, will judge you. There is appeal to social rules that should be upheld. It is considered important to be a 'good' person and to demonstrate trust, loyalty, respect and gratitude. 'One behaves properly because, in so doing, one receives the approval of others and helps maintain social order.' Examples of responses here would be that he should not steal because it is against the law, or that he should steal because it is what is expected of a good husband.

Postconventional or principled level

The subject of much debate and not widely found in empirical studies, this level represents reasoning that is based upon principles of justice, fairness, the sanctity of human life and so on. It is argued to be appropriate to break the law on occasions where the law violates a fundamental principle. An example of a response would be that Heinz should not steal the drug because by doing so he violates a principle that everyone has the right to pursue a livelihood. Another example would be that he should steal because preserving life is more important than the right to make a living.

Table A.1 Kohlberg's stages of moral development

Level 1: **Preconventional** morality

Stage 1: Punishment-and-obedience orientation	What is right is whatever others permit; what is wrong is what others punish. There is no conception of rules. The seriousness of a violation depends on the magnitude of the consequence.
Stage 2: Individualism and instrumental orientation	Rules are followed only when it is in the child's immediate interest. Right is what gains rewards or when there is an equal exchange ('you scratch my back and I'll scratch yours').

Level 2: **Conventional** morality

Stage 3: Mutual interpersonal expectations, relationships, and conformity	'Being good' means living up to other people's expectations, having good intentions, and showing concern about others. Trust, loyalty, respect and gratitude are valued.
Stage 4: Social system and conscience	'Right' is a matter of fulfilling the actual duties to which you have agreed. Social rules and conventions are upheld except where they conflict with other social duties. Contributing to society is 'good'.

Level 3: **Postconventional** morality

Stage 5: Social contract or utility and individual rights	People hold a variety of values and opinions, and while rules are relative to the group these should be upheld because they are part of the social contract. Rules that are imposed are unjust and can be challenged. Some values, such as life and liberty, are non-relative and must be upheld regardless of majority opinion.
Stage 6: Universal ethical principles	Self-chosen ethical principles determine what is right. In a conflict between law and such principles, it is right to follow one's conscience. The principles are abstract moral guidelines organized into a coherent value system.

Source: Reproduced with permission from Schaffer 1996, p.295

Bibliography

Ainsworth, M. D. S., Blehar, M., Walters, E. and Walls, S. (1978) *Patterns of Attachment.* Hillsdale, NJ: Erlbaum.

Bender, D. and Lösel, F. (1997) 'Protective and risk effects of peer relations and social support on antisocial behaviour in adolescents from multi-problem families.' *Journal of Adolescence 20,* 661–678.

Benson, P. L. (1997) *All Kids are our Kids: What Communities Must Do to Raise Caring and Responsible Children and Adolescents.* San Francisco, CA: Jossey-Bass.

Bernard, B. (1991) *Fostering Resiliency in Kids: Protective Factors in the Family, School and Community.* Portland, OR: Northwest Regional Education Laboratory.

Biehal, N., Clayden, J., Stein, M. and Wade, J. (1995) *Moving On: Young People and Leaving Care.* London: HMSO.

Bigelow, B. J. and La Gaipa, J. J. (1980) 'The development of friendship values and choice.' In H. C. Foot, A. J. Chapman and J. R. Smith (eds) *Friendships and Social Relations in Children.* Chichester: Wiley.

Bronfenbrenner, U. (1989) 'Ecological systems theory.' *Annals of Child Development 6,* 187–249.

Brooks, R. B. (1994) 'Children at risk: fostering resilience and hope.' *American Journal of Orthopsychiatry 64,* 4, 545–553.

Bryant, B. K. (1982) 'An index of empathy for children and adolescents.' *Child Development 53,* 413–425.

Coopersmith, S. (1997) *Coopersmith Self-Esteem Inventories.* Palo Alto, CA: Consulting Psychologists Press.

Cranfield, J. and Wells, H. C. (1994) *100 Ways to Enhance Self-Concept in the Classroom.* London: Allyn and Bacon.

Daniel, B. M., Wassell, S. and Gilligan, R. (1999) *Child Development for Child Care and Protection Workers.* London: Jessica Kingsley.

Dowling, E. and Osborne, E. (1985) *The Family and the School: A Joint Approach to Problems with Children.* London: Routledge.

Downes, C. (1992) *Separation Revisited: Adolescents in Foster Family Care.* Aldershot: Ashgate.

Eisenberg, N., Miller, P. A., McNally, S. and Shea, C. (1991) 'Prosocial development in adolescence: a longitudinal study.' *Developmental Psychology 27*, 5, 849–857.

Fahlberg, V. I. (1991) *A Child's Journey through Placement.* London: British Agencies for Adoption and Fostering.

Farrington, D. P. (1991) 'Childhood aggression and adult violence: Early precursors and later-life outcomes.' In D. J. Pepler and K. H. Rubin (eds) *The Development and Treatment of Childhood Aggression.* Hillsdale, NJ: Erlbaum.

Feeney, J. and Noller, P. (1996) *Adult Attachment.* Thousand Oaks, CA: Sage.

Fergusson, D. M. and Lynskey, M. T. (1996) 'Adolescent resiliency to family adversity.' *Journal of Child Psychology and Psychiatry 37*, 3, 281–292.

Fonagy, P., Steele, M., Steele, H., Higgitt, A. and Target, M. (1994) 'The Emanuel Miller Memorial Lecture 1992: The theory and practice of resilience.' *Journal of Child Psychology and Psychiatry 35*, 2, 231–257.

Fox, N. A., Kimmerly, N. L. and Schafer, W. D. (1991) 'Attachment to mother/attachment to father: a meta-analysis.' *Child Development 62*, 210–225.

Garbarino, J. (1999) *Lost Boys: Why our Sons Turn Violent and How We Can Save Them.* New York: The Free Press.

Garbarino, J., Dubrow, N., Kosteleny, K. and Pardo, C. (1992) *Children in Danger: Coping with the Consequences of Community Violence.* San Francisco, CA: Jossey-Bass.

Gilligan, R. (1997) 'Beyond permanence? The importance of resilience in child placement practice and planning.' *Adoption and Fostering 21*, 1, 12–20.

Gilligan, R. (1998) 'The importance of schools and teachers in child welfare.' *Child and Family Social Work 3*, 1, 13–26.

Gilligan, R. (1999) 'Children's own social networks and network members: key resources in helping children at risk.' In M. Hill (ed) *Effective Ways of Working with Children and their Families.* London: Jessica Kingsley.

Goldstein, A. P. (1999) *The Prepare Curriculum: Teaching Prosocial Competencies.* Champaign, IL: Research Press.

Golombok, S. and Fivush, R. (1994) *Gender Development.* Cambridge: Cambridge University Press.

Grotberg, E. (1997) 'The international resilience project.' In M. John (ed) *A Charge against Society: The Child's Right to Protection.* London: Jessica Kingsley.

Harris, P. L., Olthof, T., Meerum Terwogt, M. and Hardman, C. E. (1987) 'Children's knowledge of situations that provoke emotion.' *International Journal of Behavioural Development 10*, 319–343.

Harter, S. (1985) *The Self-Perception Profile for Children.* Denver, CO: University of Denver.

Hartman, A. (1984) *Working with Adoptive Families beyond Placement.* New York: Child Welfare League of America.

Hartup, W. W. (1992) 'Friendships and their developmental significance.' In H. McGurk (ed) *Childhood Social Development: Contemporary Perspectives.* Hove: Erlbaum.

Howe, D. (1995) *Attachment Theory for Social Work Practice.* London: Macmillan.

Howe, D., Brandon, M., Hinings, D. and Schofield, G. (1999) *Attachment Theory, Child Maltreatment and Family Support.* London: Macmillan.

Jackson, S. (1995) 'Education in care: not somebody else's problem.' *Professional Social Work,* November, 12–13.

Kohlberg, L. (1969) 'Stages and sequence: the congitive-developmental approach to socialization.' In D. A. Goslin (ed) *Handbook of Socialization Theory and Research.* Chicago: Rand McNally.

Kreidler, W. J. (1984) *Creative Conflict Resolution.* Glenview, IL: Scott, Foresman.

La Vigna, G. and Donellan, A. (1986) *Alternatives to Punishment: Solving Behaviour Problems with Nonaversive Strategies.* New York: Irvington.

Luthar, S. S. (1991) 'Vulnerability and resilience: a study of high-risk adolescents.' *Child Development 62,* 600–612.

Lynskey, M. T. and Fergusson, D. M. (1997) 'Factors protecting against the development of adjustment difficulties in young adults expose to childhood sexual abuse.' *Child Abuse and Neglect 21,* 12, 1177–1190.

McClellan, D. E. and Katz, L. G. (1992) 'Assessing the social development of young children: a checklist of social attributes.' *Dimensions of Early Childhood 21,* 1, 9–10.

Main, M. and Weston, D. R. (1981) 'The quality of the toddler's relationship to mother and to father: related to conflict behaviour and the readiness to establish new relationships.' *Child Development 52,* 932–940.

Masten, A. (1994) 'Resilience in individual development.' In M. C. Wang and E. W. Gordon (eds) *Educational Resilience in Inner-City America.* Hillsdale, NJ: Erlbaum.

Masten, A. S. and Coatsworth, J. D. (1998) 'The development of competence in favorable and unfavorable environments.' *American Psychologist 53,* 2, 205–220.

Masten, A. S., Best, K. M. and Garmezy, N. (1990) 'Resilience and development: contributions from the study of children who overcome adversity.' *Development and Psychopathology 2,* 425–444.

Parker, R., Ward, H., Jackson, S., Aldgate, J. and Wedge, P. (1991) *Looking after Children: Assessing Outcomes in Child Care.* London: HMSO.

Petersen, C. and Seligman, M. E. P. (1985) 'The learned helplessness model of depression: current status of theory and research.' In E. Beckham (ed) *Handbook of Depression: Treatment, Assessment and Research.* Homewood, IL: Dorsey Press.

Peterson, L. and Gannoni, A. (1992) *Manual for Social Skills Training in Young People with Parent and Teacher Programmes.* Melbourne: Australian Council for Educational Research; available in UK from NFER-Nelson (01236 437457).

Piaget, J. (1952) *The Origins of Intelligence in Children.* New York: International Universities Press.

Promoting Social Competence (1999) University of Dundee and the Scottish Executive. http://www.dundee.ac.uk/psychology/prosoc.htm.

Raundalen, M. (1991) *Care and Courage.* Sweden: Rädda Barnen.

Rutter, M. (1985) 'Resilience in the face of adversity: Protective factors and resistance to psychiatric disorder.' *British Journal of Psychiatry 147*, 598–611.

Rutter, M. (1991) 'Pathways from childhood to adult life: the role of schooling.' *Pastoral Care*, September, 3–10.

Schaffer, H. R. (1996) *Social Development.* Oxford: Blackwell.

Schaffer, H. R. and Emerson, P. E. (1964) 'The development of social attachments in infancy.' *Monographs of the Society for Research in Child Development 29*, 3, (whole no. 94)

Scottish Office (1999) *Social Inclusion: Opening the Door to a Better Scotland – Strategy.* Edinburgh: The Scottish Office.

Search Institute (1997) *The Asset Approach: Giving Kids What They Need to Succeed.* Minneapolis, MN: Search Institute.

Smith, C. and Carlson, B. E. (1997) 'Stress, coping, and resilience in children and youth.' *Social Service Review 71*, 2, 231–256.

Smith, P. K. and Cowie, H. (1991) *Understanding Children's Development.* Oxford: Blackwell.

Spence, S. H. (1995) *Social Skills Training: Enhancing Social Competence with Children and Adolescents.* Windsor: NFER-Nelson.

Steinberg, L. (1993) *Adolescence.* New York: McGraw-Hill.

Stone, M. (1989) *Young People Leaving Care.* London: Royal Philanthropic Society.

Terwogt, M. M. and Stegge, H. (1998) 'Children's perspective on the emotional process.' In A. Campbell and S. Mincer (eds) *The Social Child.* Hove: Psychology Press.

Thompson, R. A. (1995) *Preventing Child Maltreatment through Social Support.* Thousand Oaks, CA: Sage.

Triseliotis, J., Borland, M., Hill, M. and Lambert, L. (1995) *Teenagers and the Social Work Services.* London: HMSO.

Turner, G. (1999) 'Peer support and young people's health.' *Journal of Adolescence 22*, 567–572.

Werner, E. (1990) 'Protective factors and individual resilience.' In S. Meisels and J. Shonkoff (eds) *Handbook of Early Childhood Intervention.* Cambridge: Cambridge University Press.

Werner, E. E. and Smith, R. S. (1992) *Overcoming the Odds: High Risk Children from Birth to Adulthood.* Ithaca, NY: Cornell University Press.

Wheal, A. (1998) *Adolescence: Positive Approaches for Working with Young People.* Dorset: Russell House.

Zahn-Waxler, C., Radke-Yarrow, M. and King, R. A. (1979) 'Child-rearing and children's prosocial initiations towards victims of distress.' *Child Dvelopment 50*, 319–330.

Subject Index

accommodation away from home 37
achievement 120
    orientation 15
addiction problems 16
adult role models, positive 16
adversities 11, 157, 159
affective areas, skills in 92
aggression 91
altruism 46
ambivalent attachment 28, 36
angry face 74, 75
angry scene 80, 82
anticipate potential problems 111
antisocial behaviour 48, 91
anxious face 76, 77
anxious preoccupation 28
appearance 56, 120
appraisal 148
ashamed face 76, 77
assessment 20, 25–102
    and intervention chart 21, 22–3
athletic competence 56
attachment
    ambivalent 28
    avoidant 27, 28
    disorganised 28
    network
        wider resources contributing to young
            person's 32–3, 35
            capitalising upon 114–17
    quality of 36
    secure and insecure 27–30
    sibling 16
attention 94, 100, 152–3
attributes
    individual 96
    peer relationship 97
    social skills 96–7
see also Social Attributes Checklist
attributions 90
autonomy 16, 89, 93, 100, 149–50
    encouragement for (girls) 16
avoidant attachment (Type A) 27, 28, 36
awareness of needs, interests and feelings of
    others 66

balancing act 105–6
behaviour 120
    constructive 67
behavioural conduct 56
behavioural development 15
behavioural skills 92
bored face 76, 77

boys, encouragement for expression of feelings
    in 16
British Agencies for Adoption and Fostering
    (BAAF) 7

'cascade' model of training new volunteers 131
case studies 156–59
    interventions 156–7, 59
    messages 157, 159–60
    resilience and protective factors 158
    vulnerabilities and adversities 156, 158
cause and effect, understanding 92
Center for Sexual Assault and Traumatic Stress,
    Harborview Medical Center, Seattle 36
Centre for Child Care and Protection Studies,
    Dundee University 7
chain of coping that enables successful social
    competence 148
children, four or fewer 16
Children's Centres, North Edinburgh 7
close bond with at least one person 16
cognitive skills 37, 90, 92
comforting
    behaviour, encouraging young person to
        show 143–5
    level of shown by young person 71–2, 88
community, wider 9
competence 15
    athletic 56
    interpersonal 92
    job 56
    scholastic 56
    schooling as island of 38
conflict management/resolution, social skills in
    46, 92
conformity 162
conscience and social system 162
continuity of opportunity 57
conventional level of moral reasoning 162
cooperative play, poor social skills in 46
coping
    that enables successful social competence,
        chain of 148
    strategy
        carrying out 148
        choice of 148
        evaluating 148
Creative Conflict Resolution (Kreidler) 146

decision-making 92
dimension on which resilience can be located 11
disorganised attachment 28, 36
Dundee University 7, 89

ecological approach to intervention 106
ecological framework 9–10

ecological levels at which resilience factors can be located 9
education 14, 15, 18, 22, 37–44
    background information 37–9
    checklists
        parent/carer 42–4
        young person 40–1
    interventions 106, 157–8, 160
    opportunities in wider environment to support young person's 41, 44
        exploring 125–7
    practice suggestions for intervention strategies 120–7
    as process 39
    school/college as a place 39
educators as people 39
emotional development 15
emotional faces 74–7
emotional problems 46
emotional scenes 78–82
emotional support 45
emotion-focused coping strategy 148
empathy 15, 69–71, 87, 92
    index of, for children and adolescents 7, 83–6
        administration 83
        checklist 84
        scoring 83
            sheet 85–6
    of young persons with people close to them, helping 141–3
ethical principles, universal 162
evaluation 21
    of strategy 148
expression of feelings, encouragement for (boys) 16
external locus of control 99

family
    factors associated with resilience 16
    harmony 16
    relationships 9, 15
feelings 110
    understanding of own 69–71, 87
        helping young person 141–3
financial and material resources, sufficient 16
friend(ship)s 14, 15, 18, 23, 45–54, 89, 106, 120
    background information 45–8
    characteristics to help make and keep friends 49, 53
        helping young person to develop 128–9
    checklists
        parent/carer 53–4
        young person 49–52
    close bond of 16, 56
    helping young person's current 130–2

my friends and me as a friend (questionnaire) 51–2
    parent/carer environment facilitates development of
        encouraging 129–30
        extent 50, 53
    pleasure in 92
    practice suggestions for intervention strategies 127–32
    what are young person's friendships like at moment? 50, 54
frightened face 74, 75
frightened scene 78, 82
future, sense of 89, 94–5, 101, 153

gentleness 15
girls, encouragement for autonomy in 16
grandparents, close 16
group entry, poor social skills in 46
guilty face 76, 77

happy face 74, 75
happy scene 79, 82
health 15
helpful behaviour
    encouragement of by parent/care environment 88, 143
    required 16
    level shown by young person 71
holistic approach to intervention 106

identity 15, 65
immature perspective-taking ability 46
Index of Empathy 7
individual 10
individual attributes 96
individual rights 165
individualism and instrumental orientation 165
insecure attachment 27–30
    ambivalent (Type C) 28, 36
    avoidant (Type A) 27, 28, 36
    disorganised (Type D) 38, 36
instinctive response, ability to inhibit 92
intelligence 16
internal locus of control 15, 89, 99
    scoring 99
Internal/External Locus of Control Scale 94, 98–9
International Resilience Project 12
interpersonal competence 92
intervention 20, 103–61
    balancing act 105–6
    case studies 156–7, 158–9
    ecological approach 106
    holistic approach 106
    introduction 105

multi-agency, network approach 106–7
practice suggestions
education 120–7
friendships 127–32
positive values 141–5
secure base 107–19
social competencies 146–55
talents and interests 132–41
process of assessment and planning for 17
strategies 105–55
intimate relationships 45
'island of competence', schooling as 38

job competence 56

Kohlberg's stages of moral development 7, 162

LAC (Looking After Children) materials 15, 17, 20
learning
encouraging parent/carer environment facilitating young person's 123–5
young person's interest in 40–1, 42–3
encouraging 121–3
leisure 120

male 15
Maryhill Social Work Centre, Glasgow 7
mental health, lack of parental 16
moral development, Kohlberg's stages of 162
moral dilemma 73
moral reasoning 67
helping young person develop 141–3
level of shown by young person 69–71, 87
stages 160–3
conventional level 161, 162
postconventional or principled level 161, 162
preconventional level 160, 162
multi-agency, network approach to intervention 106–7
mutual interpersonal expectations 162

neighbour and other non-kin support 16
network approach to intervention 106–7
Nowicki-Strickland Internal/External Locus of Control Scale 98
see also Internal/External Locus of Control Scale
nurturance 15, 16

opportunity, continuity of 57

parent/carer checklist 20
people, educators as 39
peer
contact 16
relationship(s) 15
attributes 97
support initiatives 130–1
personal characteristics, extent of contribution to child's level of social competence 93–4, 100–1
perspective, ability to see others' 92
Perth Social Work Department 7
physical appearance 56, 120
planning 92
capacity 16
positive adult role models 16
Positive Approaches for Working with Young People (Wheal) 146
positive self-concept 15
positive values 14, 15, 19, 23, 65–88, 89, 106
background information 65–8
checklists
parent/carer 87–8
young person 69–72
practice suggestions for intervention strategies 141–5
postconventional level of moral reasoning 164, 165
practice suggestions for intervention strategies
education 120–7
friendships 127–32
positive values 141–5
secure base 107–19
social competencies 146–55
talents and interests 132–41
preconventional level of moral reasoning 160, 162
Prepare Curriculum (Goldstein) 146
principled level of moral reasoning 164, 165
problem-focused coping strategy 148
problem-solving 89, 92, 93–4, 100, 150–1
process, education as 39
'Promoting Social Competence' project 89, 146
prosocial behaviour 67
encouraging young person to show 143–5
level of shown by young person 71–2, 88
protective environment 11
protective factors 159
proud face 76, 77
punishment-and-obedience orientation 165
purpose, sense of 89, 94–5, 101, 153
puzzled face 76, 77

quality of attachment 36

rational thinking or reasoning 66
reflection 92, 111

relationships
  family 9, 15
  intimate 45
  mutual interpersonal expectations,
    conformity and 162
  peer 15
  supportive 39
residential care settings, giving messages to
  young people in 118–19
resilience 10–14, 45, 89, 159
  dimension on which resilience can be
    located 11
  domains of 14–15
  during adolescent years, summary of factors
    associated with 15–16
  ecological framework 9–10
  family factors associated with 16
  framework for assessment of factors 11
  individual factors associated with 15–16
  introduction to 9–16
  wider community factors associated with 16
responsibility 15
romantic appeal 56
Rosenberg Self Esteem Scale 61–2

sad face 74, 75
sad scene 81, 82
scholastic competence 56
school or college
  experiences, good 16
  facilitating young person's
    learning/attendance by parent/carer
    environment 41, 43
  encouraging 123–5
  as a place 39
  poor adjustment 46
  poor attainment 46
  young person's interest in 40–1, 42–3
    encouraging 121–3
schooling as 'island of competence' 38
Scottish Executive 7, 89
secure attachment (Type B) 27–30, 36
secure base 14, 15, 18, 22, 27–36
  background information 27–30
  checklists
    parent/carer 34–5
    young person 30–3
  ensuring young person has 112–14
  helping young person feel secure 110–12
  interventions 106, 157, 160
  practice suggestions for intervention
    strategies 107–19
  provided by parent/carer environment 31–2,
    34–5
  quality of attachment 36
  of young person 30–1, 34
self-care 15

self-control 93–4, 100, 150–1
self-efficacy 90, 100, 152
self-esteem 38, 55–6
  Rosenberg Scale 61–2
self-knowledge 45
separations, lack of 16
sharing
  behaviour, encouraging young person to
    show 143–5
  level of shown by young person 71–2, 88
shocked face 76, 77
sibling attachment 16
sociability 46
social acceptance 56
Social Attributes Checklist (McClellan and Katz)
  93, 96–7
social competence(s) 14, 15, 19, 23, 55,
  89–102
  background information 89–92
  chain of coping that enables successful 148
  checklists
    parent/carer 100–2
    young person 93–5
  encouragement of by parent/carer
    environment 95, 101
    helping 153–4
  helping young person to develop, in wider
    social environment 154–5
  helping young person to develop personal
    characteristics that help with 149–53
  Internal/External Locus of Control Scale 94,
    98–9
  interventions 106, 128, 160
  opportunities to develop in wider social
    environment 95, 101–2
  personal characteristics as contribution to
    child's level of 93–4, 100–1
  practice suggestions for intervention
    strategies 146–55
  sense of purpose and future 94, 101
  Social Attributes Checklist 93, 96–7
social contract or utility and individual rights
  165
social maturity 15
social perceptiveness 15
social presentation 15
social skills 45
  attributes 96–7
  poor 46
Social Skills Training (Spence) 146
social system and conscience 162
Social Work Services Inspectorate, Scottish
  Executive 7
Society for Research in Child Development 7
sport 120
Stop Think Do (Peterson and Gannoni) 146
stress 45, 47
structure, preference for 16

support, neighbour and other non-kin 16
supportive relationships 39
surprised face 76, 77

talents and interests 14, 15, 19, 23, 55–64
    background information 55–7
    checklists
        parent/carer 63–4
        young person 58–9
    development/expression of encouraged by
        parent/carer environment 59, 64
        ensuring 135–7
    interventions 106, 156–7, 160
    opportunities in wider environment for
        nurturing 59, 64
        drawing upon 137–41
    practice suggestions for intervention
        strategies 132–41
    of young person 58, 63
        encouraging 133–4
    what can I do and what would I like to do?
        (list) 60
temperament 94, 100, 151–2
theory of mind 66
Trinity College, Dublin 7
trust 16

understanding of own feelings 69–71, 87
    helping young person 141–3
universal ethical principles 162

values
    positive *see* positive values
    set of 16
vulnerabilities 11, 156, 158

wider community 9
    factors associated with resilience 16
willingness and capacity to plan 16
wishes and feelings 110
workbook, when and how to use 17–23
    assessment 20
    evaluation 21
    how? 18–19
    intervention 20
    parent/carer checklist 20
    when? 17–18
    young person's checklist 19

young person's checklist 19

Author Index

Ainsworth, M.D.S. 27, 163
Aldgate, J. 165

Beckham, E. 165
Bender, D. 48, 163
Benson, P.L. 65, 163
Berliner, L. 36
Bernard, B. 89, 163
Best, K.M. 90, 165
Biehal, N. 163
Bigelow, B.J. 47, 163
Blehar, M. 163
Borland, M. 166
Brandon, M. 169
Bronfenbrenner, U. 9, 163
Brooks, R.B. 29, 38, 55, 57, 163
Bryant, B.K. 83, 163

California State Department of Education 55
Campbell, A. 166
Carlson, B.E. 146, 150, 166
Chapman, A.J. 163
Clayden, J. 163
Coatsworth, J.D. 153, 165
Coopersmith, S. 56, 163
Cowie, H. 47, 65, 166
Cranfield, J. 120, 163

Daniel, B.M. 7, 11, 27, 110, 163
Donellan, A. 151, 165
Dowling, E. 120, 163
Downes, C. 28, 111, 163
Dubrow, N. 164

Eisenberg, N. 66, 164
Emerson, P.E. 166
Ennis, E. 7
Ennis, J. 7

Fahlberg, V.I. 27, 111, 164
Farmer, S. 7
Farrington, D.P. 91, 164
Feeney, J. 29, 164
Fergusson, D.M. 47, 48, 164, 165
Fine, D. 36
Fivush, R. 47, 164
Fonagy, P. 10, 29, 164
Foot, H.C. 163
Fox, N.A. 29, 164

Gannoni, A. 146, 165
Garbarino, J. 37, 153, 164
Garmezy, N. 90, 165
Gilligan, R. 7, 11, 13, 29, 37, 163, 164
Goldstein, A.P. 66, 67, 142, 146, 164
Golombok, S. 47, 164
Gordon, E.W. 165
Grotberg, E. 12, 106, 107, 164

Hardman, C.E. 164
Harris, P.L. 66, 164
Harter, S. 55, 56, 120, 164
Hartman, A. 164
Hartup, W.W. 45, 164
Henderson, C. 7
Hill, M. 166
Hinings, D. 165
Howe, D. 27, 28, 30, 46, 165

Jackson, S. 37, 38, 165
John, M. 164

Katz, L.G. 93, 96, 100, 165
Kimmerly, N.L. 29, 164
King, R.A. 67, 166
Kohlberg, L. 65, 163, 165, 165
Kosteleny, K. 164
Kreidler, W.J. 146, 165

La Gaipa, J.J. 47, 163
Lambert, L. 166
La Vigna, G. 151, 165
Lösel, F. 48 163
Luthar, S.S. 12, 55, 89, 165
Lynskey, M.T. 47, 48, 164, 165

McClellan, D.E. 93, 96, 100, 165
McGurk, H. 164
McNally, S. 164
Main, M. 29, 165
Masten, A.S. 90, 91, 105, 153, 165
Meisels, S. 166
Miller, P.A. 164
Mincer, A. 166

Noller, P. 29, 164
Nowicki, S. 98

Olthof, T. 164
Osborne, E. 120, 163

Pardo, C. 164

Parker, R. 15, 37, 165
Pepler, D.J. 164
Petersen, C. 90, 165
Peterson, L. 146, 165
Piaget, J. 37, 165
Promoting Social Competence 89, 146, 165

Radke-Yarrow, M. 67, 166
Raundalen, M. 65, 165
Rubin, K.H. 164
Rutter, M. 10, 37, 166

Schafer, W.D. 164
Schaffer, H.R. 7, 45, 47, 67, 91, 165, 166
Schofield, G. 165
Scottish Office 37, 166
Search Institute 68, 166
Seligman, M.E.P. 90, 165
Shea, C. 164
Shonkoff, J. 166
Smith, C. 146, 150, 166
Smith, J.R. 163
Smith, P.K. 47, 65, 166
Smith, R.S. 11, 65, 89, 166
Spence, S.H. 146, 166
Steele, M. 164
Stegge, H. 66, 166
Stein, M. 163
Steinberg, L. 90, 163, 166
Stone, M. 46, 166

Target, M. 164
Terwogt, M.M. 66, 164, 166
Thompson, R.A. 45, 46, 47, 116, 166
Triseliotis, J. 46, 47, 57, 166
Turner, G. 130, 166

Wade, J. 163
Walls, S. 163
Walters, E. 163
Wang, M.C. 165
Ward, H. 165
Wassell, S. 7, 11, 163
Wedge, P. 165
Wells, H.C. 120, 163
Werner, E. 11, 27, 45, 65, 89, 166
Weston, D.R. 29, 165
Wheal, A. 146, 151, 166
Willshaw, D. 7
Wilson, A. 7
Wosu, H. 7

Zahn-Waxler, C. 67, 166